OLD TESTAMENT GUIDES

General Editor

R.N. Whybray

EZRA AND NEHEMIAH

D1453589

EZRA and NEHEMIAH

H.G.M. Williamson

Published by JSOT Press
for the Society for Old Testament Study

For Laura, Halcyon and Nathan,
who say it's their turn

Copyright © 1987 Sheffield Academic Press

Published by JSOT Press
JSOT Press is an imprint of
Sheffield Academic Press
The University of Sheffield
343 Fulwood Road
Sheffield S10 3BP
England

Typeset by Sheffield Academic Press
and
printed in Great Britain
by Billings & Sons Ltd
Worcester

British Library Cataloguing in Publication Data

Williamson, H.G.M.
    Ezra and Nehemiah.—(Old Testament guides,
    ISSN 0264-6498)
    1. Bible. O.T. Nehemiah—Commentaries
    2. Bible. O.T. Ezra—Commentaries
    I. Title   II. Society for Old Testament
                        Study
    III. Series
    222'.8077   BS1365.3

    ISBN 1-85075-065-3

CONTENTS

PREFACE

The invitation to contribute to the 'Old Testament Guides' series came while I was preparing a substantial commentary on Ezra and Nehemiah for the Word Biblical Commentary series. As I anticipated then, it has been a refreshing challenge to bring together a number of points which had inevitably to be scattered through a large commentary and to try to express them in a simple and clear manner. Should this book fall into the hands of those more advanced in the study of the Old Testament than the undergraduate readers for whom it is intended, I would urge them to refer to the larger work for more detailed substantiation of the conclusions reached here.

The first draft of the book was kindly typed for me by Mrs Judith Hackett. It was then carefully read both by two second year theological students (Jolyon Mitchell and Pete Wilcox) and by the series editor, Professor R.N. Whybray. To all these (and especially the last-named) I am grateful for suggestions about how to express more clearly the various matters under discussion.

H.G.M. Williamson
Cambridge
December 1985

ABBREVIATIONS

ANET	J.B. Pritchard (ed.), *Ancient Near Eastern Texts relating to the Old Testament* (3rd edn), Princeton: Princeton University Press, 1969
AOS	American Oriental Series
AP	A. Cowley, *Aramaic Papyri of the Fifth Century B.C.*, Oxford: Clarendon Press, 1923
BA	*Biblical Archaeologist*
BWANT	Beiträge zur Wissenschaft vom Alten und Neuen Testament
BZ (N.F.)	*Biblische Zeitschrift* (neue Folge)
BZAW	Beihefte zur *ZAW*
CBQ	*Catholic Biblical Quarterly*
EvQ	*Evangelical Quarterly*
FRLANT	Forschungen zur Religion und Literatur des Alten und Neuen Testaments
IDBSup	K. Crim *et al.* (eds.), *The Interpreter's Dictionary of the Bible, Supplementary Volume*, Nashville: Abingdon, 1976
JBL	*Journal of Biblical Literature*
JNES	*Journal of Near Eastern Studies*
JSOT	*Journal for the Study of the Old Testament*
JSS	*Journal of Semitic Studies*
JTS (n.s.)	*Journal of Theological Studies* (new series)
NEB	*New English Bible*
OTS	*Oudtestamentische Studiën*
RB	*Revue biblique*
RSV	*Revised Standard Version*
RVV	Religionsgeschichtliche Versuche und Vorarbeiten
SVT	Supplements to VT
VT	*Vetus Testamentum*
ZAW	*Zeitschrift für die alttestamentliche Wissenschaft*
ZDPV	*Zeitschrift des deutschen Palästina-Vereins*

Select List of Commentaries

P.R. Ackroyd, *I & II Chronicles, Ezra, Nehemiah* (Torch Bible Commentaries), London: SCM Press, 1973. Suitable for beginners, this commentary is particularly valuable for its treatment of literary and theological themes.

R.A. Bowman, 'Introduction and Exegesis to the Book of Ezra and the Book of Nehemiah', *The Interpreter's Bible*, vol. 3, New York and Nashville: Abingdon Press, 1954, 551-819. Apart from the value of its detailed comments, this work is useful for non-German-speaking readers in that it frequently follows Rudolph's approach (see below).

D.J.A. Clines, *Ezra, Nehemiah, Esther* (New Century Bible), Grand Rapids: Wm.B. Eerdmans and London: Marshall, Morgan & Scott, 1984. A fine and up-to-date commentary, replacing the less satisfactory work by L.H. Brockington in the same series. Its clear summaries of major critical issues and its balanced discussion make this probably the best single commentary for student readers.

R.J. Coggins, *The Books of Ezra and Nehemiah* (The Cambridge Bible Commentary), Cambridge: Cambridge University Press, 1976. Based on the NEB, this brief commentary is useful for preliminary orientation.

F.C. Fensham, *The Books of Ezra and Nehemiah* (The New International Commentary on the Old Testament), Grand Rapids: Wm.B. Eerdmans, 1982. Whilst this commentary includes many helpful matters of detail, it is disappointing in terms of its lack of attention to the historical and theological results of literary analysis.

F.D. Kidner, *Ezra and Nehemiah* (Tyndale Old Testament Commentaries), Leicester: IVP, 1979. The exegesis in this little commentary gives much thought-provoking food for reflection. A series of six appendices sets out some of the major critical issues and tries to deal with them in a responsible manner from a conservative point of view.

J.M. Myers, *Ezra, Nehemiah* (Anchor Bible), Garden City: Doubleday, 1965. For want of anything better, this has served a generation of scholars as the standard English-language critical commentary. It is strongest in the fields of historical analysis and setting, particularly with regard to lists and the like.

H.E. Ryle, *The Books of Ezra and Nehemiah* (The Cambridge Bible for Schools and Colleges), Cambridge: Cambridge University Press, 1897. This commentary never fails to surprise by the amount of detail it has managed to pack in and by its perception of broader issues which many more recent works have overlooked. It is the best commentary by far amongst the older English-language ones, and is still worth consulting alongside more modern treatments.

H.G.M. Williamson, *Ezra, Nehemiah* (Word Biblical Commentary), Waco: Word Books, 1985. Readers will find here a more detailed defence of many of the positions necessarily summarized in the present book.

The major foreign-language commentaries include:

A. Bertholet, *Die Bücher Esra und Nehemia* (Kurzer Hand-Kommentar zum Alten Testament), Tübingen: J.C.B. Mohr, 1902.

G. Hölscher, 'Die Bücher Esra und Nehemia', in E. Kautzsch and A. Bertholet (eds.), *Die heilige Schrift des Alten Testaments* (4th edn), Tübingen: J.C.B. Mohr, 1923. These two older commentaries deserve mention because of the significant contributions which they both made towards the development of modern approaches to the literary analysis of Ezra and Nehemiah.

F. Michaeli, *Les livres des Chroniques, d'Esdras et de Néhémie* (Commentaire de l'Ancien Testament), Neuchâtel: Delachaux & Niestlé, 1967. The major commentary in French.

W. Rudolph, *Esra und Nehemia* (Handbuch zum Alten Testament, Tübingen: J.C.B. Mohr, 1949. This is arguably the finest commentary ever to have been written on Ezra and Nehemiah. It has certainly lasted as the major starting point for all subsequent serious research.

H. Schneider, *Die Bücher Esra und Nehemia* (Die heilige Schrift des Alten Testaments), Bonn: Peter Hanstein, 1959. A substantial commentary in a Roman Catholic series which has not generally received the attention it deserves.

INTRODUCTION

There is a long-running debate among teachers of the Old Testament about the best place to begin. What should be the starting point in the syllabus? Some believe, for instance, that historical background is a vital first requirement whilst others reply that since we can only reconstruct history from the literary sources we should start by examining the latter. Others suggest that a study of the prophets makes for a more attractive introduction. However, the student then quickly discovers the need for some acquaintance with the Pentateuch (who were the 'Deuteronomists' and why do scholars date them later than some of the prophets?). On the other hand, although the Pentateuch might seem to be the logical place to start, many experience great difficulty in coming to terms with source analysis and its apparently radical conclusions for the early history of Israel.

The present book is written in the belief that there is a good deal to be said for starting near the end of the Old Testament period —with Ezra and Nehemiah. On the one hand, much of the earlier part of the Old Testament can now be taken at face value because it would have already reached its present shape by this later time. On the other hand, no one doubts that the author here had access to sources, and in some cases there is no great difficulty in determining more or less what they were: Nehemiah's first-person account of his own activities is an obvious example. However, if we are willing, as we should be, to follow through the logical results of such an analysis we quickly discover that it has an important bearing on our reconstruction of the history of the period, and especially of the order in which things took place. And from there, of course, it is only a short step to asking why, then, the editor has arranged things as he has, a question which demands a more ideological and theological response.

This is not to suggest that scholars are in complete agreement concerning Ezra and Nehemiah; far from it! Part of our purpose will be to outline and, if possible, evaluate some of the many proposals which have been advanced on the more important controversial points. Nevertheless, it should emerge clearly that there is no real alternative to the kind of methods of study which are under discussion if we wish to work responsibly with the text as we have it. It is to be hoped, therefore, that from this guide to a part of the Old Testament where some of these issues are at their clearest readers may come to feel more comfortable with them and so begin to learn an approach to study which will give them a smoother passage into other more complicated areas.

Readers should be advised that there is one drawback to the method being pursued here, namely that the first chapter is likely to prove the toughest reading. Discussion of sources and the like demands quite a close look at the material, so that those who are not familiar with the outline of Ezra and Nehemiah may need to take some time to read this chapter in close conjunction with the text. In itself, this is no bad thing—after all, this book is intended as a guide to, not a replacement for, Ezra and Nehemiah. Nevertheless, I hope that the discussion will prove to be intelligible and that the reward of increased understanding when we get to the later chapters will more than compensate for the initial investment of time and effort.

CHRONOLOGICAL CHART

Persian Kings[*]		*Main events in Judah*	
		538-522	Various returns from exile under Sheshbazzar, Zerubbabel and others(?) (Ezra 1-2)
559-529	Cyrus (539/38: capture of Babylon and authorization of temple rebuilding)		
		538/7 (?)	Altar dedication (Ezra 3.1-6)
529-522	Cambyses		
522-486	Darius I Hystaspes	520-515	Building of the second
486-465	Xerxes I		temple (Ezra 5-6)
465-425	Artaxerxes I Longimanus	458	Traditional date for Ezra's mission (Ezra 7-10; Neh. 8)
		448 (?)	Abortive attempt to rebuild the walls (Ezra 4.7-23)
		445-433	Nehemiah's first term as governor (Neh. 1-7)
		438/428	Alternative dates for Ezra's mission
		430 (?)	Nehemiah's second term as governor (Neh. 13)
425-424	Xerxes II		
424	Sogdianus		
424-405	Darius II Ochus		
405-359	Artaxerxes II Memnon	398	Main alternative date for Ezra's mission
359-338	Artaxerxes III Ochus	332	Judah comes under Hellenistic rule
338-336	Arses		
336-331	Darius III Codomannus		

[*]Based on I. Gershevitch (ed.), *The Cambridge History of Iran*, vol. 2 (Cambridge: University Press, 1985)

1

SOURCES

THE BOOKS of Ezra and Nehemiah divide into sections which for the most part are clearly and easily defined. Ezra 1–6 describes the circumstances surrounding the return of a number of Jews from their place of exile in Babylon and their efforts, which were eventually successful, to rebuild the temple in Jerusalem. Ezra 7–10 follows at an unspecified interval, though a new king, Artaxerxes, has now succeeded the Cyrus and Darius of chs. 1–6. This Artaxerxes authorizes 'Ezra the priest, the scribe of the law of the God of heaven' (7.12) to go to Jerusalem with treasures for the temple and a commission to undertake teaching of the law and reform. Once there, however, Ezra learns of the marriage of a number of Jews to foreign wives; his response is to establish a commission which leads to the divorce of these wives.

With the start of the book of Nehemiah, the scene shifts back again to the community in exile and the date is some thirteen years later in the reign of (the same?) Artaxerxes. Hearing of the plight of his fellow Jews in Jerusalem, Nehemiah makes use of his position as royal cup-bearer to secure permission to journey there in order to rebuild the city. In the event it is the walls which he rebuilds in the teeth of external opposition and not a little internal unrest (Neh. 1–6).

So far, each section has followed the pattern of a return from exile and some measure of reform or restoration. The final part of the book of Nehemiah is less straightforward. It includes material about the repopulation of Jerusalem in Nehemiah's time (Neh. 7 and 11), the dedication of the newly-built city wall (12.27-43), and various incidents related to Nehemiah's second term as governor (ch. 13). Interspersed with this, however, are a presentation of the law by Ezra followed by a confession of sin by the people and their pledge to keep the law in future (Neh. 8-10) as well as various lists of residents of Jerusalem, priests, Levites and others in Neh. 11.3-12.26.

With this outline sketch in mind, we are in a position to begin to ask how we are to make sense of this varied material. We shall need, for instance, to take account of the fact that two of the chief characters (Ezra and Nehemiah) each apparently tell part of their tale in their own words, while of the remainder some is in Hebrew and some in Aramaic, a language closely related to Hebrew and used as a 'diplomatic language' in the Persian empire (Ezra 4.8–6.18; 7.12-26).

It is apparent that this wide variety of material is due to the use of different sources by whoever compiled these books into their present shape. If we can isolate what these sources were, we shall be in a stronger position to trace not only how they have been stitched together but why this has been done in the way that it has. We shall start with the easiest source to isolate, the first-person account of Nehemiah.

A. The Nehemiah Memoir

1. *Extent*

The following passages in the book of Nehemiah appear to be a first-hand account by Nehemiah himself: chs. 1-2 (preparation and return to Jerusalem); 4-6 (rebuilding of the walls in spite of difficulties); 7.1-5 (defence of the city and start of a move to repopulate Jerusalem); parts of 12.31-43 (dedication of the wall); and 13.4-31 (Nehemiah's second term as governor). This material is characterized by lively narrative and forceful style and in particular by some idiosyncratic turns of phrase, especially the interjected prayers that God will 'remember' Nehemiah for good or his enemies for ill (cf. 5.19; 6.14; 13.14, 22, 29 and 31).

These passages cannot, however, be read as a single and coherent narrative. There are some gaps in the account, especially at chapter 7, where the account of Nehemiah's attempt to repopulate Jerusalem is broken off short. This shows that the Nehemiah source must once have been more extensive than it is now. Can we, then, isolate any more material which once belonged to it?

In ch. 3 there is a long list of those who participated in the wall-building. It is unlikely that Nehemiah originally compiled this list because it displays a number of differences from his own account. For instance, it looks back at the completion of the work, including the gates (e.g. vv. 1, 3, 6 etc.), whereas later on 6.1 explicitly states that this stage had not yet been reached. Furthermore, Nehemiah does not refer to himself here, although he may be mentioned obliquely as 'their lord' in v. 5. Nevertheless, there is no reason why Nehemiah should not have *included* this independent list in his account. Apart from the fact that the list reflects creditably on his abilities as a leader and organizer, the narrative at the end of ch. 2 and again at the beginning of ch. 4 seems to presuppose its inclusion.

Far more controversial is the list of names in 7.6-73. In the verses just before, Nehemiah states that to help him encourage more Judaeans to live in Jerusalem he found 'the genealogy of those who came up at the first'. There then follows this list which, not surprisingly, turns out to be the same as the list in Ezra 2. Probably the majority of scholars doubt whether Nehemiah would have included it in his account. On the other hand, it can be argued that modern literary sensibilities may not apply to a writer of antiquity and that 7.5 half leads us to expect a list; the issue is thus best left open.

Despite the reference to Nehemiah in 8.9, chs. 8–10 are quite obviously not part of his own account. In fact, the question of repopulating Jerusalem in 7.5ff. is only picked up again at the start of ch. 11. Since ch. 11 is not written in the first person, however, most commentators believe that this is a portion of the memoir which was rewritten by a later editor. This suggestion, however, is improbable. Apart from the very different style of writing, 11.1-2 does not really fit with ch. 7. There, Nehemiah is all set to deal with the problem on the basis of family lists whereas here in 11.1 it is decided on the arbitrary basis of casting lots. It is thus best to conclude that here is evidence that we have lost part of Nehemiah's account (and if so, how much else has been lost without trace?), and that some alternative account of the affair has been included instead.

A similar conclusion applies to the passage about the dedication of the wall, 12.27–43. Though the narrative comes to a satisfactory conclusion on this occasion, those who try to follow the story line in detail will soon find that certain points necessary for understanding it do not appear, whilst other material unrelated to Nehemiah (e.g. vv. 27–30) has been interspersed with it. Finally, the present setting of the passage arouses suspicion: would it not more naturally fit at the completion of the wall-building in ch. 6?

When we turn to ch. 13, we find that we have jumped over at least twelve, and probably more, years (compare the date in 13.6 with 1.1, and cf. 5.14). Also, the 'remember' formula suddenly becomes more frequent, and the focus of Nehemiah's attention switches more to the realm of religious practice.

It is not difficult to see why there is general agreement that the book of Nehemiah includes an authentic first-person account by Nehemiah of his activities relating to Jerusalem. However, our survey has also revealed some curious features which require an explanation. Just what sort of a document is it that we are dealing with here?

2. *Genre*

Although we have followed the convention of referring to the 'Nehemiah Memoir', that is obviously inappropriate as a technical literary classification. It was Mowinckel who first pointed this out, and he suggested instead that the work might more appropriately be compared with a number of ancient Near Eastern royal inscriptions in which various kings may commemorate their achievements (English translations in *ANET*). Von Rad later endeavoured to refine Mowinckel's thesis by comparing the Memoir instead to various tomb and temple inscriptions from Egypt (English translations in Lichtheim). These date from roughly the same period as Nehemiah and recall in first-person narrative the duties of senior officials faithfully performed, often in spheres of public life which closely resemble those of Nehemiah.

A third approach takes the distinctive 'remember' formula as its starting point and finds the closest parallels to the Nehemiah Memoir in the common votive or dedicatory inscriptions known in several Aramaic dialects from later times (cf. Cooke), though earlier examples are also known (e.g. *ANET*, p. 653). Curiously, although this view is often mentioned in introductory textbooks, it has not been worked out in a full-scale study. The disparity in length between Nehemiah's account and these brief inscriptions has thus never been faced or explained.

Another suggestion is that Nehemiah needed to write in order to justify himself for one reason or another to the Persian king. Based more on the contents of the text than on formal analogies with other sources, this view suggests that accusations had been levelled against Nehemiah by some of his opponents. A major difficulty which proponents of this view have not been able to deal with satisfactorily is that the document appears to be addressed directly to God rather than to the king.

Finally, in the most recent major study of Nehemiah, Kellermann starts from a position similar to that just outlined, but then adduces the type of psalm known as the 'Prayer of the Accused' in order to explain the distinctive characteristics of the Nehemiah material. The obvious differences between these two bodies of literature are explained by the particular circumstances in which Nehemiah was placed.

Here, then, are five principal attempts to explain what the Nehemiah Memoir is, but none has succeeded in commanding general assent. Kellermann's criticisms of the first four proposals are frequently apposite: he finds that none does justice to all the evidence. They each fit one part well while ignoring or contradicting another. Meanwhile, his own suggestion has been shown to raise even greater problems (see Emerton's review).

In the face of such difficulties, it is surely in order to ask whether the problem does not lie in trying to categorize under a single heading material which really does not belong together. Consider the following points :

(a) There is a long and unexplained gap between the wall-building and related events on the one hand and ch. 13 on the other. Chapter 13 describes various reforms undertaken by Nehemiah during his second term as governor, and this must have been well over twelve years after the start of his first term (compare 5.14 and 13.6). It is impossible to believe that after a first year's frenetic activity Nehemiah did nothing worthy of note for the remaining eleven years of his first term as governor!

(b) Whilst it is clearly important to take account of the 'remember' formula, it is peculiar to find that none refers to the wall-building. It would be a strange votive inscription, however defined, which did not offer the supplicant's major achievement as a reason why God should remember him.

(c) All the points which Nehemiah asks God positively to remember must come from at least twelve years after Nehemiah's arrival in Jerusalem. This is clear for ch. 13, which is set in Nehemiah's second term as governor. The same is true for 5.19. This verse summarizes the short paragraph 5.14-19, and 5.14 states explicitly that it refers to the whole of Nehemiah's first term as governor, a period of twelve years.

These observations suggest the probability that the Nehemiah Memoir developed in two quite distinct stages. Without the paragraphs (all quite short) which ask God to remember Nehemiah, everything centres on the wall-building and fits into a short space of time. In 2.6, Nehemiah records that 'it pleased the king to send me; and I set him a time'. This suggests that his original commission was specific (to build the wall) and comparatively short—certainly not twelve years! There is no reason, therefore, to doubt that the substance of the Nehemiah story has at its base a report on how this short-term commission was fulfilled.

Very much later, Nehemiah reworked this report in votive style. He may have felt that justice was not being done to him in his own community, because all the points which he asks God to remember are included in the separate account of a pledge which the people undertook in Neh. 10 (see below). He thus added a few short paragraphs which had the effect of altering the whole atmosphere of his earlier report into an appeal to God to have his good deeds in remembrance. No doubt at this stage too it would have been rendered into Hebrew and some other additions made (e.g. the prayer in ch. 1). The result represents a mixture of literary types. It is thus not surprising that attempts to compare it as a whole with other unified texts have never proved fully convincing.

Further Reading

Apart from commentaries (see above, pp. 9-10), the major works on the Nehemiah Memoir are all in German:

> S. Mowinckel, *Studien zu dem Buche Ezra-Nehemia. II: Die Nehemia-Denkschrift*, Oslo: Universitetsforlaget, 1964. In this monograph Mowinckel reworked material that he had first presented in Norwegian as early as 1916
> G. von Rad, 'Die Nehemia-Denkschrift', *ZAW* 76 (1964), 176-87
> U. Kellermann, *Nehemia. Quellen, Überlieferung und Geschichte* (BZAW 102), Berlin: Töpelmann, 1967. English-speaking readers will find a full summary and discussion of this work in the detailed review by J.A. Emerton, *JTS* n.s. 23 (1972), 171-85

English translations of ancient texts with which the Nehemiah Memoir has been compared may be found in the following :

> G.A. Cooke, *A Text-Book of North-Semitic Inscriptions*, Oxford : Clarendon, 1903
> M. Lichtheim, *Ancient Egyptian Literature. A Book of Readings*,

Volume III: The Late Period, Berkeley: University of California, 1980
J.B. Pritchard (ed.), *Ancient Near Eastern Texts relating to the Old Testament*, 3rd edn, Princeton: Princeton University, 1969

B. The Ezra Material

1. *The Problems*

Material in which Ezra plays a major role is found in Ezra 7-10 and Neh. 8. It looks at first sight as though Neh. 9-10 are a direct continuation of this, but Ezra is not mentioned in the Hebrew text of these two chapters (despite the RSV of 9.6), and so a first difficulty to be faced is where they come from originally.

A second curious feature about the Ezra story is the way it switches between passages in the third person (7.1-26; 8.35-36; 10; Neh. 8) and the first person (the whole of Ezra 7.27-9.15 apart from 8.35-36). Was it written like this from the start, and if so why, and by whom? Or did an editor have in front of him Ezra's own account from which he copied some parts but rewrote others? And again, since it is difficult to detect an individual style of writing in these chapters, in contrast with the case of Nehemiah, what evidence is there that would enable us to speak of a 'source' at all?

Finally, the order of events is odd. Taking the text as it stands, Ezra came to Jerusalem in the seventh year of Artaxerxes (cf. 7.7-8) with a commission, amongst other things, to teach and implement the law of God (7.25-26). Within a year, he dealt with the problem of mixed marriages (chs. 9-10), but he then waited another full twelve or thirteen years before getting round to presenting the law in fulfilment of his original commission (Neh. 8, apparently in the twentieth year of Artaxerxes, following the dates of Neh. 1.1; 6.15, and 8.2). This gap in Ezra's career has never been satisfactorily explained.

Here, then, is an inter-related group of problems, both literary and historical. Clearly, the first step towards unravelling them will be to assess how these chapters came to be written.

2. *Survey of Opinions*

Our difficulties are not eased by the welter of conflicting opinions which scholars have voiced concerning this material. For simplicity's sake, they may be classified into four groups.

(a) *C.C. Torrey*. Whilst until the end of the nineteenth century the

Ezra material was generally taken at face value, Torrey then subjected it to the most searching criticism in a brief monograph and a subsequent succession of articles. Because of its Hebrew style, he concluded that it could not be distinguished from the editorial hand of the author who, he and many others believed, was responsible for the whole of the work comprising Chronicles, Ezra and Nehemiah, generally known as 'the Chronicler'. Therefore, he concluded, there was no separate Ezra source: Ezra was no more than a figure of the Chronicler's fiction.

Torrey's views, though much discussed, were not followed by many in their entirety. There was, however, one aspect of his analysis which attracted widespread support. He argued that the Ezra material was originally written in the order Ezra 7-8; Neh. 8; Ezra 9-10; Neh. 9-10, and that its present order was the result of mistakes by later copyists. Of course, Torrey was obliged to think this because in his view the chapters had been written from scratch by the editor of the books as a whole. If he had believed that they lay before the editor as some sort of an independent source, he might equally well have concluded that the editor had rearranged them into their present order for purposes of his own. This is a subject to which we shall have to return.

(b) *M. Noth and A.S. Kapelrud.* Writing in obvious independence of each other during the second world war, the German scholar Noth and the Norwegian Kapelrud both came to comparable conclusions, though on somewhat different grounds. Literary and historical considerations led Noth to believe that the edict of Artaxerxes in Ezra 7.12-26 and the list in 8.1-14 of those who accompanied Ezra on his journey to Jerusalem were both sources which were available to the Chronicler. The Chronicler also knew the Nehemiah Memoir. On the basis of this material, the Chronicler himself wrote the whole of the Ezra account. This suggestion explained why the style so closely resembled the Chronicler's, why Neh. 8 appears where it does (the Chronicler wrote it for that setting for theological reasons), and why part of the account is in the first person (inconsistent imitation of Nehemiah).

Kapelrud, meanwhile, undertook a study of the Hebrew style of the Ezra narrative. Like Torrey, he concluded that it must be attributed to the same hand as the Chronicler, but at the same time he allowed the probability that some earlier tradition underlay the account. Kapelrud was not as specific as Noth about this, however, and his stylistic analysis is also open to criticisms of method. It is not surprising, therefore, that it is Noth's form of this theory which has had the most influence, especially on the more recent major studies of Kellermann and of In der Smitten. The attraction of this approach is that it enables scholars to discount the possibility of an Ezra source while nevertheless holding on to the historicity of Ezra himself.

(c) *S. Mowinckel.* As in the case of his work on the Nehemiah material, Mowinckel first published on Ezra in 1916 in Norwegian, but his views only became generally accessible by way of a German monograph in 1965. His opinion is more conservative than that of Noth, but paradoxically it is far from traditional. Finding some editorial comments in the Ezra material, Mowinckel argues that this editor is the Chronicler. Therefore, he must have been working on an already existing text—an Ezra source. Mowinckel can find no reason, however, to attribute this to Ezra. It was, he thinks, the work of an admirer who had been a young man during Ezra's activity, and who years later wrote up an idealized version of the events for purposes of edification. Since history was not its main aim, allowances should be made for all manner of legendary embellishment. Needless to say, Mowinckel had no difficulty in citing other examples of narratives which use the first-person singular but which are not auto-biographical.

(d) *Traditional.* Despite the arguments of the scholars whose views have just been summarized, there have continued to be many, led by Rudolph in his fine commentary, who have held to a more traditional approach. That is to say, they accept that the material about Ezra was originally written by Ezra in the first person throughout in order to give an account of his work to the Persian king, who had commissioned him. It was later reworked by the Chronicler, who among other things cast some of it into the third person. However, since Torrey's time all but the most conservative, such as Kidner and Fensham, have agreed that Neh. 8 (and perhaps 9–10) was once an integral part of the Ezra material in Ezra 7–10. Opinions are divided over the question whether its present position is the result of accident or design.

3. *Evaluation*

In trying to pick a pathway through these various opinions, the first point to be made is that in today's climate the argument from Hebrew style cannot be regarded as decisive either way. New discoveries and improved research since Torrey's day have increased our awareness of the extent to which the Hebrew language developed during the Old Testament period. The Babylonian exile in particular was a watershed, since after that time the influence of Aramaic and Iranian as well as other factors left a clear mark on the Hebrew language. Now, though the amount of Hebrew of post-exilic origin in the Bible is relatively limited, we still know enough to be able to say that a good deal of what Torrey and others attributed to the style of the Chronicler turns out in fact to be no more than the general style of the period. Clearly, this has first to be discounted. When we then look at what remains, it becomes apparent that the style of the books of Chronicles and of the Ezra material is by no means so even as to compel us to believe that it is necessarily the product of a single hand. Arguments along this line are thus best set aside—a conclusion of no small significance in view of the prominent part which, as we have seen, they play in the history of this inquiry.

Turning, then, to considerations of a more general literary and historical nature, we should start by examining the relationship between the edict of Artaxerxes and the subsequent narrative. Are the connections so close as to suggest that the latter has been written up solely on the basis of the former, as Noth and others maintain? In some respects, this is a possibility. The studied emphasis on the care with which the gifts for the temple were handled is a case in point (cf. 7.15-20; 8.24-30, 33-34). However, the climax of the edict comes in 7.25-26 with the command to 'appoint magistrates and judges who may judge all the people in the province Beyond the River, all such as know the laws of your God', but there is not so much as a whisper of this being fulfilled. It is thus difficult to see how the Ezra narrative can be no more than a 'midrash' on the edict.

Coupled with this are a number of points of detail, such as place names (8.15, 17), an inventory (8.26-27), curious local colour (10.9, 13) and an unexpected hitch in the preparations for the journey (8.15ff.) which are clearly not based on the edict but which also have no other apparent origin than historical memory. Again, we shall argue later that Neh. 8 originally stood between Ezra 8 and 9, and that it has been moved to its new position for positive theological reasons. If so, then an editor must have been working with an inherited source rather than composing from scratch.

Finally, what are we to say about the switches from first to third person and vice versa? The most obvious explanation is that an editor, working on an original first-person account by Ezra, changed some passages into the third person. He no doubt considered that it was appropriate to introduce Ezra in this way (7.1-10). He then used the words of Ezra's benediction (7.27-28) as a skilful way to slip over into the first person. He continued with this throughout chs. 8 and 9 with the exception of 8.35-36, where he may have been 'papering over' the gap caused by his transfer of material to Neh. 8. Then at the end of ch. 9 he again used the device of prayer to revert to the third person both because it was more suitable to round off this section of his work and because there is evidence that he rewrote this last part more extensively (e.g. the wording of 10.3 and 16 suggests that he may have omitted some material; it is likely that he abbreviated the list in 10.18ff.; some material may have been moved from 10.15-16 to the start of Neh. 9, as we shall see later). Finally, Neh. 8 had obviously to be in the third person to avoid confusion with Nehemiah.

Mowinckel's response to this 'common sense' approach is not as convincing as at first appears. In trying to argue that the text included third- and first-person material from the start, he draws attention to other texts which he believes are parallel in this respect. Closer examination reveals, however, that in most cases they are first-person texts with a third-person introduction or heading. This, of course, is quite normal (e.g. Neh. 1.1!). When we look for texts which switch back and forth, however, we find that what few examples there are are definitely later than Ezra, and that the best parallel, the book of Tobit, has probably been directly influenced by Ezra. It remains most likely, therefore, that these unprecedented changes in person point to the work of an editor on a source that goes back to Ezra himself.

What purpose might such a source have originally fulfilled? If it is accepted that Neh. 8 originally belonged between Ezra 8 and 9, then it is suggestive that the dates in the material about Ezra are spread out evenly over a period of exactly twelve months. Moreover, it has already been noted that there is a conscious attempt to match the terms of Artaxerxes' edict with the account of what actually happened. Of its four stipulations, two are carried out to the letter: the leading to Jerusalem of any Jews who wished to go, and the transportation and delivery of various gifts and grants to the temple. The third stipulation—'to make inquiries about Judah and Jerusalem according to the law of your God' (7.14)—is perhaps picked up in

10.16-17 to suggest that this too was carried out, though not quite as at first expected. The fourth stipulation, as we have seen, was not fulfilled, though Neh. 8 points to the start of a teaching ministry. On the basis of these observations, and with the Nehemiah material as a parallel, it is not unreasonable to suggest that, as a matter of regular protocol, Ezra was obliged to report on his progress after one year. Naturally, he will have gone as far as he could to show how he fulfilled the terms of his commission, a fact which explains the present account better than the theory of a pious and idealizing biographer. That a copy of such a text should have been available later in Jerusalem and that an editor should have worked it over when he included it in a larger composition is no cause for surprise.

Further Reading

The major works in English on the Ezra material are:

C.C. Torrey, *The Composition and Historical Value of Ezra-Nehemiah* (BZAW 2), Giessen: Ricker, 1896

C.C. Torrey, *Ezra Studies*, Chicago: University Press, 1910 (reprinted New York: KTAV, 1970)

M. Noth, *The Chronicler's History* (JSOT Supplement Series, 50), Sheffield: JSOT Press, 1987 (a translation of part of *Überlieferungsgeschichtliche Studien 1*, originally published in 1943)

A.S. Kapelrud, *The Question of Authorship in the Ezra-Narrative. A Lexical Investigation*, Oslo: Dybwad, 1944

K. Koch, 'Ezra and the Origins of Judaism', *JSS* 19 (1974), 173-97

P.R. Ackroyd, 'The Chronicler as Exegete', *JSOT* 2 (1977), 2-32

To gain a full view of scholarly opinion, however, the following works in German and the major commentaries (especially Rudolph and Williamson) should be added:

H.H. Schaeder, *Esra der Schreiber*, Tübingen: Mohr, 1930

F. Ahlemann, 'Zur Esra-Quelle', *ZAW* 59 (1942-43), 77-98

S. Mowinckel, *Studien zu dem Buche Ezra-Nehemia III: Die Ezra-Geschichte und das Gesetz Moses*, Oslo: Universitetsforlaget, 1965

Kellermann, *Nehemia*, esp. 56-69

W. Th. In der Smitten, *Esra: Quellen, Überlieferung und Geschichte* (Studia Semitica Neerlandica 15), Assen: Van Gorcum, 1973

In the modern period, the question of style has been discussed by:

R. Polzin, *Late Biblical Hebrew. Toward an Historical Typology of
  Biblical Hebrew Prose* (Harvard Semitic Monographs 2),
  Missoula: Scholars Press, 1976
H.G.M. Williamson, *Israel in the Books of Chronicles*, Cambridge:
  University Press, 1977, 37-59
M.A. Throntveit, 'Linguistic Analysis and the Question of
  Authorship in Chronicles, Ezra and Nehemiah', *VT* 32
  (1982), 201-16

C. **Other Material in Nehemiah**

We have already seen that only a limited part of the second half of the
book of Nehemiah can have come from his memoir. It has also been
noted that ch. 8 probably originated in the Ezra source. We must
therefore now briefly survey the remaining chapters. It should be
remembered that at this preliminary stage we are looking at the
question of sources and so must concentrate on what *distinguishes*
one passage from another. Later on, of course, we shall also be
discussing the contribution which each makes to the book as we now
have it, regarded as a new and unified literary whole.

1. *Nehemiah 9* relates how after Ezra's presentation of the law the
people assembled again to be led by the Levites in a long prayer of
confession. Many commentators believe that this chapter too was
once part of the Ezra Memoir, and they tend to think that it
originally followed the settlement of the mixed marriages affair in
Ezra 10.
    In fact, however, the leading thoughts of the prayer are so
diametrically opposed to those of Ezra that it cannot ever have been
associated with him. To give just one example, Ezra's attitude to the
Persian kings was extremely positive: the revival of the Jewish
community was due to their benevolence under God's inspiration; cf.
Ezra 7.6, 27-28; 9.9. The contrast with the sentiments of Neh. 9.36-
37 could hardly be more complete. The fact that, again in complete
contrast with Ezra 9, there is no mention here of exile and
restoration but only of the people having suffered one defeat after
another in the land (cf. vv. 26-30) suggests that this prayer may have
originated in the circle of those Judaeans who were never sent into
exile in Babylon but who continued to live in Palestine.
    The narrative introduction in vv. 1-4, however, with its talk of the

Israelites 'separating themselves' from foreigners, of 'the seed of Israel' (v. 2, obscured by RSV) and of the book of the Law is much more at home in Ezra's world; compare especially Ezra 9.1-2 (and note that RSV's 'holy race' is literally 'holy seed'). Perhaps, then, the substance of these few verses originally came between Ezra 10.15 and 16. It fits that context well, and it might explain why the Hebrew text of v. 16 became corrupted. But, of course, this is only a suggestion.

2. *Nehemiah 10* (including 9.38 in the English versions) again divides into two parts—a solemn undertaking by the people to keep God's law in general (v. 29) and in several specific details which are spelled out (vv. 30-39) on the one hand, and a list of those who signed this pledge (vv. 1-26) on the other. Because this list interrupts a single sentence in the Hebrew (Hebrew 10.1 and 30b; English 9.38 and 10.29b), it must clearly have been added to an already existing text. It may have been the original list of those who signed, moved here by the editor, but for various reasons it is more likely, in my opinion, that it is his own compilation, aiming to show how the whole community united to sign this pledge which, as we shall see, comes at a major climax of the work.

As for the pledge itself, it seems originally to have been an independent document. Scholars have rightly been impressed with the fact that its stipulations agree closely with the subject matter of Neh. 13, Nehemiah's second term as governor:

mixed marriages	10.30;	13.23-30
Sabbath observance	10.31;	13.15-22
the wood offering	10.34;	13.31
firstfruits	10.35-36;	13.31
Levitical tithes	10.37-38;	13.10-14
neglect of the temple	10.39;	13.11

This close similarity leaves us with two possibilities. (a) After these abuses had been exposed and Nehemiah had taken steps to deal with them, the community made an agreement that they would not happen again. (b) After the community had agreed to observe a series of stipulations, precisely these points of the law were later abused. The first of these two possibilities is clearly the more probable. Accordingly, from a historical point of view Neh. 10 followed after Neh. 13.

3. *Nehemiah 11.1-20.* We observed when discussing the Nehemiah Memoir that, contrary to popular opinion, 11.1-2 does not belong to the Memoir, but is of independent origin. There is no good reason then to doubt that the substance of the following list in vv. 3-20 rests on an authentic record of those who lived in Jerusalem after the city's population had been supplemented. There is a parallel to this list in 1 Chron. 9. This helps to confirm that the tidy conclusion to the list in v. 20 was once its ending; at the same time the differences between the two passages show the extent to which changes could come in during the course of transmission. There is nothing more that we expect after 11.1-2 than what we find in 11.3-20.

4. *Nehemiah 11.21-12.26.* The various lists in this section are probably later additions to the basic composition of this section. After the satisfactory conclusion in v. 20, v. 21 supplements v. 3, v. 22 supplements vv. 15-18, v. 23 supplements v. 22, and v. 24 supplements v. 23. By this time, the original tidy list was becoming obscured, and it is not surprising that the opportunity should have been taken to expand the passage still further with lists of settlements, priests, Levites and the like. Since this is a late and secondary process, we need not trace it further here—a fortunate conclusion since the process was more than usually complicated.

5. *Nehemiah 12.27-13.3.* As previously noted, Nehemiah's own account of the dedication of the wall has been interspersed with some other material—material which seems to take a particular interest in the role of the cult officials. The remaining verses of this section are of very uncertain origin. Most attribute 12.44-47 to the editor himself, whilst 13.1-3 may record some separate commitment of the people along lines similar to the pledge in ch. 10.

6. *Conclusions.* As we look over this apparent jumble of material, two features stand out. Of the passages in the book of Nehemiah which Nehemiah did not himself write from scratch, many show a particular interest in the temple and its personnel: the list of wall-builders in Neh. 3 is headed by the high priest and his fellow priests, and it starts and ends at the Sheep Gate, which gave access to the temple. The pledge in Neh. 10 ends with a note of strong support for the temple, and v. 39a, which is probably a secondary addition, is likely to have been added with a similar concern in view. 'Lot-

casting', as recorded at the start of ch. 11, was a cultic affair at this time (cf. 1 Chron. 24.5, 7, 31; 25.8, 9; 26.13, 14 and especially Neh. 10.34), and we have noted that the alternative account of the dedication of the wall is marked by similar interests. It is thus reasonable to suppose that much of this material was drawn by the editor from the temple archives.

The second striking feature about this material is the extent to which it parallels many of Nehemiah's personal accomplishments in both the secular and the sacred realms. Wall-building, repopulation of Jerusalem, rectification of religious abuse and wall-dedication—for each of these we have both a personal account by Nehemiah and an account in which the people as a whole under priestly leadership are more prominent. This, it may be suggested, dovetails with our earlier conclusion about the two-stage growth of the Nehemiah Memoir: Nehemiah was determined that his contribution in these areas should not be overlooked, and so he worked over his earlier report in order precisely to draw attention to his contribution in these other spheres.

Further Reading

These chapters have not previously been made the subject of any specific study apart from what is to be found in commentaries. The following is a list of the major studies of the individual passages and chapters :

Torrey, *Ezra Studies*, 252-84

A.C. Welch, *Post-Exilic Judaism*, Edinburgh and London: Blackwood, 1936

A. Jepsen, 'Nehemia 10', *ZAW* 66 (1954), 87-106

M. Rehm, 'Nehemias 9', *BZ* N.F.1 (1957), 59-69

S. Mowinckel, *Studien zu dem Buche Ezra-Nehemia I: Die nachchronistische Redaktion des Buches. Die Listen*, Oslo: Universitetsforlaget, 1964

U. Kellermann, 'Die Listen in Nehemia 11 eine Dokumentation aus den letzten Jahren des Reiches Juda?', *ZDPV* 82 (1966), 209-27

Kellermann, *Nehemia*

D. Ezra 1-6

The opening chapters of the book of Ezra have an historical setting many years prior to the work of Ezra and Nehemiah, for they tell of the first return of Jewish exiles from Babylon and the rebuilding of the temple. They are also unlike the chapters studied so far, in that there is no obvious major source which provides a framework for the whole passage, although many scholars believe that the lengthy section in Aramaic (4.6–6.22) was already put together as a source before it was used by our author.

When we come in the next chapter to look at how these books were put together, we shall find that there are alternative explanations which have an important bearing on the question of sources. In order not to get embroiled in that now, we shall here simply go through what look like, or purport to be, the 'raw materials' in this section, the 'original sources' out of which any longer composition must have developed. For clarity's sake, rather than following the biblical order, we shall start with the less controversial items.

1. *The inventory of temple vessels (1.9-11).* There is general agreement that this list is based on an authentic source. The use of obscure vocabulary of apparently Aramaic origin and other linguistic oddities point strongly to this, whilst the general form is of a type known from elsewhere (cf. *AP* 61 and 63). Since our knowledge of such lists suggests that it would once have had an introduction, stating who gave what to whom, and when, it becomes likely that the introduction here too (vv. 7-8) is a paraphrase of this material. The use of a Persian word for 'treasurer' and of the Persian name 'Mithredath' in v. 8 supports this conclusion.

This little passage is thus very instructive. It shows us not only that the author had access to primary sources, but also that, on this occasion at least, they determined the way in which he wrote his 'history'. He did not introduce sources to illustrate his account which he derived from somewhere else; rather, he knew only as much as these sources told him. This is illustrated particularly in the present case by the fact that he obviously knew nothing about the return from Babylon itself, beyond that it happened (cf. 1.11b). With this, we may contrast ch. 8, where Ezra gives us full details of his comparable journey, *including* a similar inventory (8.26-27).

2. *The list of those who returned (ch. 2).* No one seriously doubts that this long list lay in front of our author as a source. It was therefore not unreasonable that he should have used it to fill in for his lack of an account of the return of the exiles from Babylon. Whether that

was its original purpose, however, may be doubted. It is curious, for instance, that following in the wake of ch. 1 there is no reference to Sheshbazzar or the temple vessels which he transported. Again, the list seems to have been drawn up from the perspective of those already living in the land rather than journeying to it: the people all have their own towns to live in and 'the governor' (v. 63) seems already to be installed in his work. Further investigation also suggests that the list has been built up out of several separate items. In particular, several different ways of grouping the laity are used in vv. 3-35.

Quite why this list was originally compiled is uncertain. Suggestions have been made that it was for purposes of taxation or the distribution of land, but there is little evidence for this. More attractive is Galling's proposal: he notes that during the building of the second temple some twenty years after the first return the Jews were obliged to supply a list of names of all who were officially permitted to take part in the work (cf. 5.3-4, 10). He suggests that this is a copy of that list. If so, it would be interesting to include Japhet's recent proposal that the list purposely amalgamates those who had been in exile with those who had remained in the land— these latter being those identified by their place of residence in vv. 21-35. She sees in this a desire to gather into one all who were loyal adherents to the Jerusalem cult as the community of 'exiles', whether they had been in Babylon or not.

Speculative as these latter suggestions must inevitably be, we may conclude that we have here some kind of a register of the first generation of members of the post-exilic Judaean community. It cannot be used, however, to settle the issue whether they all returned at once, or whether what we have here is not rather the telescoping of a number of groups who came to Jerusalem during the first two decades of Persian rule.

3. *Some letters in Aramaic (4.6–6.12)*. The bulk of this lengthy passage comprises what purport to be the transcripts of letters between local officials and the Persian court. They raise several interrelated questions: Are the letters authentic or fabricated? Were they already joined together into an Aramaic source before they reached our author, or did he work direct from the originals? And how are we to explain the order of the material, in view of the fact that the Artaxerxes of ch. 4 reigned long after the Darius of chs. 5–6?

Some of these problems will be more easily treated in the next chapter. The general question of authenticity, however, should be considered here.

As so often with such matters, the major issues at stake were already defined at the end of the last century, with Torrey denying the authenticity of these letters and E. Meyer defending them with equal vigour. It might be supposed that the use of Aramaic, the fact that in 4.6 and 7 exchanges of letters are alluded to but not cited verbatim, and the assurance from Haggai and Zech. 1–8 that the temple was indeed rebuilt early in the reign of Darius would all create a presumption in favour of the genuine nature of these letters. Why, then, have they aroused suspicion? First, because it is thought that the form of Aramaic in which they are written is later than the sixth–fifth century BC; second, because it is considered improbable that a Persian king would have shown such detailed interest in the Jerusalem temple (see, for instance, 6.3-4); and, third, because of the suspiciously Jewish wording of some passages (e.g. 6.9-10 and 12).

In a splendid article first published in 1937, de Vaux outlined a response to these objections; more recent discoveries and research have generally supported his conclusions. As regards the language, it is true that some of the *spellings* in Ezra are more modern than contemporary papyri known to us, but the language itself remains the same. Our knowledge of Aramaic has increased significantly since de Vaux first wrote because of the publication of many new texts. Now that we can see the extent to which Aramaic changed later on, the general agreement of the language in Ezra with the earlier papyri is underlined. At the same time, however, it has now become clear that the Aramaic of the Persian period could differ from place to place, as is only to be expected. Minor differences between various groups of texts can thus no longer be so immediately used for dating purposes.

Regarding general historical probability, de Vaux drew on a wide range of first-hand evidence to demonstrate that concern for and support of local cults by the Persian kings was quite characteristic of their policy. The best-known example of this is the Cyrus Cylinder (cf. *ANET*, 315-16), in which Cyrus both attributes his victory over Babylon to the Babylonian god Marduk and orders the restoration of several local cults. It is true that in their haste to defend the biblical account some scholars have pressed this evidence further than is justified (cf. Kuhrt), but even without this the objection to these letters on historical grounds remains unproven.

Finally, to the literary objections, de Vaux responded (like Meyer before him) that in all probability Jews were engaged in the Persian administration to draft appropriate replies. Indeed, we can go even further than this: we know from elsewhere, especially Elephantine and Xanthos, that such documents were sometimes drafted as a response to a petition by the local population, and that in responding the local officials naturally adopted much of the wording from the petition itself.

If de Vaux effectively countered the criticism levelled against these letters, the most recent work has gone further in positively championing their authenticity. There are now enough Aramaic letters known from the period to permit form-critical comparisons of such matters as address, greeting, transition and other formulae, and so on. Without entering into detail, it may be said that to a remarkable degree the text of these letters fits into this pattern, and further that the narrative introductions to them include just the kind of information which we would expect to have been included in the address, subscript and summary of contents. The force of this argument is strengthened by the fact that later Greek letter-writing practices were quite different. It is thus hard to suppose that these letters would have been 'forged', as a few have alleged, so late as the Hellenistic period.

4. *The decree of Cyrus (1.2-4)*. The last apparent source in Ezra 1–6 to be considered is the decree in Hebrew which Cyrus wrote, authorizing the Jews to return to Jerusalem in order to rebuild the temple. Many more doubts have been cast upon this decree, even by scholars, such as de Vaux, who defend the authenticity of the Aramaic letters.

First, the use of Hebrew is a clear difficulty. Would Cyrus have used this very local language? And if not, why did the author not leave this text in Aramaic, as he did on other occasions? Second, the historical, religious and literary problems seem to many to be even stronger here than in the letters. For instance, there is no first-hand evidence that Cyrus ever referred to himself as 'king of Persia'. Finally, the memorandum of Cyrus in 6.3-5 seems to many to provide the clue: our author used that Aramaic text as a basis for his own free composition.

These objections are undoubtedly weighty and have persuaded

many. It would be wrong, however, to give the impression that there
is nothing to be said on the other side. Bickerman especially has
replied to a number of the specific objections along lines similar to
those noted in connection with the Aramaic letters. I would add three
further points.

First, 1.2-4 cannot have been based on 6.3-5, for the latter says
nothing about a return of Jews, which is the main point of 1.2-4, and
conversely 1.2-4 says nothing about the specifications of the temple,
which is the main point of 6.3-5.

Second, 1.2-4 is presented in a particular form, known as a
'message'. It is not a formal decree, but something addressed directly
to a specific audience. In that case we could guess that it was a
message addressed to the Jewish leaders in exile. This might help
explain its language and style.

Third, there are some differences between 1.2-4 and the
surrounding narrative which make us question whether they were
both written by the same author. The first verse, for instance,
announces Cyrus's message as a universal proclamation—an evident
theological interpretation. Again, if those translators of ancient and
modern times are right who render v. 4 'And those who remain
behind who belong to any of the places where he is living shall help
him . . . ', then there is a difference from v. 6. The decree would be
urging Jews who stayed in exile to give material help to those who
were going. Verse 6, however, influenced no doubt by Exodus
typology and the theme of 'despoiling the Egyptians' (cf. Exod. 3.21-
22; 11.2; 12.35-36; Ps. 105.37), interprets this in terms of support by
Gentile neighbours.

We may thus conclude that there is a possibility that 1.2-4
represents a source which the author used and that, as we have seen
earlier, he based his narrative directly on it. The case is not certain,
and some of the phraseology still makes it look as though at best any
original record has passed through Jewish hands. Interestingly,
however, without this passage in front of him, our author would not,
so far as we can judge, have had any source at all from which to
derive the idea of a return in the first place. And yet that there was
such a return seems certain in view of the well-attested tensions
which developed later between the returning exiles and the local
population.

Further Reading

The main collections of Aramaic letters which may be compared with those in Ezra 1–6 are:

AP

G.R. Driver, *Aramaic Documents of the Fifth Century B.C.*, Oxford: Clarendon, 1957

J.C.L. Gibson, *Textbook of Syrian Semitic Inscriptions II: Aramaic Inscriptions*, Oxford: Clarendon, 1975, 125-43

For form-critical discussions of these texts, see

P.S. Alexander, 'Remarks on Aramaic Epistolography in the Persian Period', *JSS* 23 (1978), 155-70

P.-E. Dion, 'Les types épistolaires hébréo-araméens jusqu'au temps de Bar-Kokhbah', *RB* 96 (1979), 544-79

J.A. Fitzmyer, 'Aramaic Epistolography', *A Wandering Aramean: Collected Aramaic Essays* (SBL Monograph Series 25), Missoula: Scholars Press, 1979, 183-204.

J.L. White (ed.), *Studies in Ancient Letter Writing*. Semeia 22 (1982)

On the Aramaic of this period, see

J. Naveh and J. Greenfield, 'Hebrew and Aramaic in the Persian Period', in *The Cambridge History of Judaism*, I, 115-29. There is a bibliography on pp. 421-25

E.Y. Kutscher, 'Aramaic', in *Encyclopaedia Judaica*, vol. III, 259-87

E.Y. Kutscher, 'Aramaic', in T.A. Seboek (ed.), *Current Trends in Linguistics*, VI, The Hague: Mouton, 1970, 347-412

J.D. Whitehead, 'Some Distinctive Features of the Language of the Aramaic Arsames Correspondence', *JNES* 37 (1978), 119-40

On Ezra 1:

E.J. Bickerman, 'The Edict of Cyrus in Ezra 1', *Studies in Jewish and Christian History*, Part One, Leiden: Brill, 1976, 72-108

K. Galling, *Studien zur Geschichte Israels im persischen Zeitalter*, Tübingen: Mohr, 1964, 61-88

A. Kuhrt, 'The Cyrus Cylinder and Achaemenid Imperial Policy', *JSOT* 25 (1983), 83-97

On Ezra 2:

K. Galling, 'The "Gōlā-List" According to Ezra 2// Nehemiah 7', *JBL* 70 (1951), 149-58

S. Japhet, 'People and Land in the Restoration Period', in G. Strecker (ed.), *Das Land Israel in biblischer Zeit*, Göttingen: Vandenhoeck & Ruprecht, 1983, 103-25

Mowinckel, *Studien I*, 29-45; 62-109

C. Schultz, 'The Political Tensions Reflected in Ezra- Nehemiah', in C.D. Evans, W.W. Hallo and J.B. White (eds.), *Scripture in Context*, Pittsburgh: Pickwick, 1980, 221-44

Other:

E. Meyer, *Die Entstehung des Judenthums*, Halle: Niemeyer, 1896

R. de Vaux, 'The Decrees of Cyrus and Darius on the Rebuilding of the Temple', in *The Bible and the Ancient Near East*, London: Darton, Longman & Todd, 1972, 63-96

H.G.M. Williamson, 'The Composition of Ezra i-vi', *JTS* n.s. 34 (1983), 1-30

2

COMPOSITION
AND DATE

HAVING SURVEYED the building blocks, so to speak, of Ezra and Nehemiah, we must move on to examine how they have been assembled into their present shape. Following our discussion in Chapter 1, it will come as no surprise to learn that there are various views about this, and that they differ considerably in matters of detail. Here, however, we can deal only with the broad outlines of these suggestions.

A. The Chronicler and Ezra-Nehemiah

The most widely held view, at least until recent times, has been that the books of Ezra and Nehemiah are a direct continuation of the books of Chronicles (note the overlap between 2 Chron. 36.22-23 and Ezra 1.1-3). It is therefore believed that the Chronicler himself was responsible for the arrangement of the sources in Ezra-Nehemiah and for writing the connecting narrative material. Some of these sources (e.g. the Aramaic material in Ezra 4–6 and perhaps even the memoirs of Ezra and Nehemiah themselves) may have been joined before his time, and some material, especially in the latter part of Nehemiah, is often thought to have been added later, but this does not affect the major conclusion that Ezra and Nehemiah as we have them are broadly speaking an integral part of the work of the Chronicler.

On this view, some of the difficulties which the books pose can be explained away. The exchange of letters in Ezra 4.7-23, for instance, is chronologically out of place: Artaxerxes reigned later than Darius, and hence this passage ought to come after Ezra 6 at the earliest. But the Chronicler, it is held, was not a particularly good historian when

judged by modern standards. Not knowing the correct order of the
kings of Persia, he mistakenly believed that these verses furnished an
explanation for the delay in building the second temple (cf. Ezra 4.4–
5 and 24) and so relocated them accordingly.

It is also considered possible that, if the dates of Ezra and
Nehemiah have been confused (cf. ch. 3 below), responsibility for
this should again be laid at the door of the Chronicler, either because
he knew no better or because he wanted to give particular emphasis
to Ezra the religious reformer. This, of course, ties in well with the
opinion of those who ascribe much of the material about Ezra
directly to the Chronicler.

The major source of disagreement between scholars who adopt
this general approach concerns the overlap which we have already
noted between the careers of Ezra and Nehemiah. Many believe that
this is the result of a serious mistake by later copyists. The account of
Ezra reading the law (Neh. 8) originally stood between Ezra 8 and 9,
but for one reason or another it was accidentally misplaced to its
present position. It then attracted to itself Neh. 9–10, which originally
followed Ezra 10. No conclusions should then be drawn from the
present arrangement about the Chronicler's theology or purpose in
writing. Others, however (most recent among them Clines, pp. 11–
12), are content to ascribe the present ordering of the material
directly to the Chronicler.

B. 1 Esdras

The main alternative to the view just summarized also believes that
the Chronicler played an important role in the composition of Ezra
and Nehemiah. However, the original ending of the Chronicler's
work is thought to be represented by the shape it takes in the
apocryphal book 1 Esdras. Much later this was subjected to a
substantial revision and amplification to give Ezra and Nehemiah
the form which they now have.

1 Esdras (confusingly called 3. Esra in German!) is known to us
only in its Greek form. It is mainly, however, a translation of 2
Chron. 35–36; Ezra; and Neh. 8.1-12. There are some differences in
the order of events in the early chapters of Ezra and an additional
section (1 Esd. 3.1–5.6) in which Zerubbabel's journey to Jerusalem is
introduced as a reward for his wise words in 'the contest of Darius's
bodyguards'. However, if matters such as these are ignored as

secondary, then it is suggested that 1 Esdras gives us a clue as to how the Chronicler's work 'originally' ended, namely with the book of Ezra + Neh. 8 (Ezra's reading of the law). This furnishes a satisfying account of the restoration of the temple and its cult, concluding with a religious reform not unlike those which the Chronicler described in the reigns of Hezekiah (2 Chron. 29–30) and Josiah (2 Chron. 35).

Only long afterwards, on this view, was the Nehemiah memoir incorporated into the book together with the rest of the material in the book of Nehemiah. This process itself may have been accomplished in more than one stage.

A discussion of all the problems relating to 1 Esdras would clearly be out of place in the present book. It will be enough for the moment merely to deal with two questions: (1) Is it likely that Neh. 8 was ever the direct continuation of Ezra 10? (2) Does 1 Esdras betray any knowledge of other parts of Nehemiah? If (as I believe) the answer to the first question is 'no' and to the second is 'yes', then clearly we shall have to conclude that 1 Esdras does not represent the 'original' ending of the Chronicler's work but that it is a later, separate composition which has selected and arranged its material for reasons of its own. (These reasons may not be easy to determine, since it is likely that 1 Esdras is a fragment which has lost both its beginning and its conclusion.) This view has an *a priori* attractiveness in that it no longer becomes necessary to indulge in special pleading to explain the inclusion of 1 Esd. 3.1–5.6 and the different order of the events of Ezra 1–4.

That Neh. 8 belonged originally with Ezra 7–10 is doubted by hardly anyone. (The reference to Nehemiah in v. 9 is a later addition.) Ezra, not mentioned in the preceding chapters, suddenly becomes the centre of attention, while the dates in 7.73 and 8.2, which use numbers for the month ('the seventh month'), correspond with Ezra's usage (cf. Ezra 7.8–9; 8.31; 10.9, 16–17) whereas Nehemiah always refers to the months by name (e.g. Chislev in Neh. 1.1, Nisan in 2.1 and Elul in 6.15). Where, then, within Ezra 7–10 does Neh. 8 fit best?

As we noted already in Chapter 1, Torrey was the first scholar to pose this question, and his answer was clear: Neh. 8 belongs between Ezra 8 and 9. Amongst his reasons were the observations that Ezra came to Jerusalem specifically to present and teach the law, so that a reading of the law ought to come early in Ezra's ministry; that the dates in the Ezra material fit smoothly in sequence on this view (the

seventh month of Neh. 8 follows the fifth month in which Ezra
arrived at Jerusalem and precedes the ninth-tenth months in which
the problem of mixed marriages was dealt with; cf. Ezra 7.9 and
10.16); and that Ezra 9 seems to presuppose knowledge of the law by
the people. Torrey has been followed in his conclusion by the
majority of subsequent commentators.

Those who argue, by contrast, that Neh. 8 once followed
immediately after Ezra 10 generally do so because of their prior
convictions about 1 Esdras. The result is that they do not present
positive reasons to favour their view, but merely seek to explain away
the difficulties which it raises, principally the odd sequence of events
and their respective dates. Nor do they help their case by emphasizing
that Ezra's law was not completely new—as though the alternative
view demanded that it was! On balance, therefore, it seems more
likely that Neh. 8 was never joined to Ezra 10, in which case 1 Esdras
must be a quite secondary compilation.

The second question posed above regarding 1 Esdras was whether
it betrays any knowledge of parts of Nehemiah which are supposed to
have been added only later. Several such have been suggested (and of
course any one would be fatal to the priority of 1 Esdras), but not all
are by any means totally convincing. There is one, however, which
cannot be ignored, for it both disposes of the value of 1 Esdras as
evidence for an earlier stage in the development of Ezra-Nehemiah
and provides a clue for a more satisfactory composition history.

Ezra 2 comprises a long list of those who returned from the exile in
Babylon. Exactly the same list is repeated in Neh. 7.6ff., where
Nehemiah cites it as the basis on which he intended to move some of
the population into Jerusalem. The very slight differences between
the two forms of the list (e.g. variations in numbers) are nearly all to
be explained as later scribal slips.

When we look more closely at the end of the list, we find a striking
phenomenon: the parallel wording runs on well beyond the conclusion
of the list itself and into the following narrative. Ezra 3.1 is almost
word for word the same as Neh. 7.73b–8.1. However, in both cases,
the parallel sentence introduces the next story (dedication of the altar
in Ezra 3; Ezra's reading of the law in Neh. 8). This means that the
list cannot have been copied independently at both places from some
common original source because that hypothesis would not explain
this further narrative overlap. Rather it must be that Ezra 2 has
copied directly from Neh. 7 or vice versa; the question is, which?

For several good reasons, the majority opinion is that Ezra 2 has been copied from Neh. 7. (i) In Ezra 3.1, the date ('the seventh month') does not relate to anything; it hangs completely in the air. In Neh. 7.73b, however, it fits perfectly—both with 'the first day of the seventh month' in Neh. 8.2 following, and, as we have already seen, with the whole scheme of dates in the account of Ezra's work. (ii) As was pointed out earlier, the way that the month is numbered ('the seventh month') is typical of Ezra's priestly style, and as such it contrasts with Nehemiah's. We can now add, however, that it also contrasts with the rest of Ezra 1–6, where the narrator usually relates events to a given year of the king (e.g. 1.1; 4.24; 6.15) or some other fixed occasion (e.g. 3.8). Nowhere else do we find an unattached numbered month, as at 3.1. This looks, therefore, as though it comes originally from Ezra. (iii) The variations in the figures at the end of the list can best be explained if Ezra 2 has summarized Neh. 7; the reverse process makes no sense. As the text is not in good order, I set out the two passages as commentators agree they should be restored:

Ezra 2.68-69	Neh. 7.70-72
When they arrived at the temple of the Lord in Jerusalem, some of the heads of families gave freewill offerings towards the rebuilding of the temple of God on its original site. According to their means they gave to the fund for this work 61,000 drachmas of gold, 5,000 minas of silver and 100 priestly vestments.	Some of the heads of families gave to the work. The governor gave to the treasury 1,000 drachmas of gold, 50 bowls, 30 priestly vestments, and 500 minas of silver. Some of the heads of families gave to the treasury for the work 20,000 drachmas of gold and 2,200 minas of silver, while the remainder of the people gave 20,000 drachmas of gold, 2,000 minas of silver and 67 priestly vestments.

From this we may observe, for instance, that in the matter of priestly vestments Neh. 7 has 30 + 67 items, and that Ezra 2 has rounded this up to 100, while for silver minas the sum in Neh. 7 is 500 + 2,200 + 2,000 which Ezra 2 has rounded up to 5,000. If the dependence had been the other way round, we should certainly have expected the totals in Ezra 2 to be divided accurately in Neh. 7. We may conclude for these and other reasons that Ezra 2 borrowed directly from Neh. 7.

The significance of this conclusion will at once become clear when it is remembered that the end of Neh. 7 is precisely the point where the sources about Ezra and Nehemiah were joined. Ezra 2–3.1, it emerges, has borrowed from both sources and must, therefore, have known them in their combined form. Thus 1 Esdras, which includes the Ezra material, cannot have come into existence before the Nehemiah memoir was incorporated into the work. It follows that we should not use it further in discussing the composition history of Ezra and Nehemiah.

C. **A Fresh Approach**

In our examination of 1 Esdras, we have stumbled across something which, though long known to scholars, has not in my opinion been given sufficient weight in the study of Ezra-Nehemiah. If Ezra 2/3 is dependent upon Neh. 7/8, then the Ezra and Nehemiah memoirs must have been joined together *before* the books reached their present final form. Thus, whereas the usual views, which we have just outlined, agree that the incorporation of the Nehemiah material was one of the latest phases in the books' composition, it seems preferable to regard it, rather, as one of the earliest.

The reason why this logical conclusion has been ignored is the prevailing assumption that the Chronicler was responsible for much of the editorial work in these books, and especially in Ezra 1–6. The thought that these chapters could be later than the rest of the work was excluded *a priori*. If we free ourselves from this presupposition, however, then we may allow the evidence to lead where it will.

We begin, then, with the joining together of the Ezra and Nehemiah memoirs (i.e. approximately Ezra 7–10 and Neh. 1–7; 8; 12.31-43 and 13.4-31). A moment's thought will reveal that most of the other material in Nehemiah must also have been included at this stage. For instance, even though Neh. 11 is not, we have argued, part of the Nehemiah memoir, it is clearly intended to serve as the narrative continuation of Neh. 7.4-5, and so it must have been put in place at the same time as Nehemiah's own account was curtailed. Similarly, it is likely that the combination of sources in the account of the dedication of the walls (Neh. 12.27-43) took place at the same time.

The most important part of this editor's work, however, was his assembling of Neh. 8–10. So far, we have discovered that each of these three chapters has its own independent origin and that the core of Neh. 8 has been moved from its original position in the Ezra memoir. But the result of this assemblage is not merely a jumble of bits and pieces. The various elements have, rather, been put together in a way that creates a pleasing overall theological unity. Ignoring the details which sometimes sit uneasily with each other, the major elements in these chapters are: proclamation of the law—confession—renewal of commitment to the covenant with general and specific stipulations. Without getting bogged down in the issue whether this was a purely literary device or whether it corresponded to some historical or cultic actuality, it may be reasonably affirmed that the editor intended this to be read as a covenant renewal. His motivation for splicing together the Ezra and the Nehemiah sources then becomes transparent: after telling of the major reforms of each, he has pulled these chapters together to form a united climax to their work. The proclamation of God's law is granted only to the purified community, while their response in confession and commitment represents the culmination of all that the reformers had been striving towards.

The second major phase in the books' composition will have been the prefacing of Ezra 1–6. In our first chapter above, we managed to isolate a number of sources, and it may now be suggested that the editor worked directly from these to his present text. The main evidence for this suggestion is that often the narrative sections which link these sources together are based directly on the wording of the sources themselves: see, for instance, 1.5-6 in relation to 1.1-4; our comments earlier on 1.7-11; the narrative of 5.3-5, which is taken from the report in the letter of 5.7-17; and the follow-up in 6.13ff., which simply records the carrying out of the king's orders in the letter of 6.2-12. Second, other parts of the narrative (e.g. 4.6-10; 5.6 and 6.1) give just the type of information which an editor could have learnt from the addresses and summaries which were regularly included in Aramaic letters of the time. We can almost picture him with a copy of each letter, extracting from it and recording as much detail of its circumstances as possible. Third, this suggestion offers the easiest explanation for the obvious lack of balance in the narrative. For instance, despite the elaborate anticipation in Ezra 1, there is no actual record of the return of the Jews from Babylon to Jerusalem. Again, in chs. 5–6 there is no detail given of the rebuilding of the temple, only of Tattenai's enquiry and its aftermath. In these and similar cases, we lack anything approaching a contemporary record or chronicle; the whole shape of the narrative is determined by what happens to have survived of official documents. Finally, most of the material not already covered can be readily explained by an editor's knowledge of earlier Biblical books (e.g. Haggai and Zechariah for Ezra 5.1-2 and 6.14) and by his assuming that things will have been done then very much as they were in his own day (e.g. Ezra 6.19-22). For the one apparent exception to this procedure (i.e. Ezra 3), see Chapter 3 § B below.

An advantage of this approach to Ezra 1–6 is that it helps to explain a major difficulty in these chapters, namely the chronology of chapter 4. The problem here is that the exchanges of letters with Xerxes (Ahasuerus) and Artaxerxes in 4.7-23 do not seem to fit the context, which refers to the earlier king Darius both before (4.5) and after. There are two main possibilities to explain this, both compatible with our approach. The first is simply to assume that the editor lived so long after the events concerned that he did not know the correct order and so mistakenly believed that the second temple was completed in the reign of Darius II rather than Darius I (see, for instance, Noth's careful discussion of this possibility).

There are, however, problems which confront this approach. On the one hand, Ezra 6.14 suggests that the editor may indeed have known that Artaxerxes came after, not before, the Darius who issued a decree concerning the temple building. The second is that the exchange of letters in 4.7ff. explicitly deals with the walls of Jerusalem and not the temple, and we have no reason to suppose that the editor would have been confused about such an obvious distinction as this when he came to write 4.24.

An alternative possibility, therefore, is to take seriously the constraints under which the editor was working. On the view being explored here, Ezra 7ff. already lay before him in its completed state. Now, if he had in front of him copies of letters from Artaxerxes' reign which he wished to include, he could not put them in their proper chronological setting, because the events in question come down to a point later than the start of the Ezra material. Faced with this dilemma, he looked for a place where he could incorporate them in a way that would make a positive contribution to his presentation. He chose their present setting because he believed that they would help explain and justify the apparently harsh rejection of the northerners' offer of assistance in 4.1-3 and show how that group's successors were indeed 'adversaries of Judah and Benjamin' (4.1; note how 4.2 and 10 forge a link between the two groups).

In a modern work, such a digression might be effected by the use of brackets or a footnote. These devices not being available to an author of antiquity, he used instead a technique known as 'repetitive resumption'. Ezra 4.24 resumes the narrative flow of 4.5 by partly repeating its wording. In this way, the material in between is marked out as being digressionary (note the clear use of the same device at 2 Chron. 12.2a and 9 by comparison with the parallel passage in 1 Kgs 14.25-28). This whole process makes admirable sense on the supposition that the editor of Ezra 1-6 worked in the manner we have suggested.

D. **Date**

There is no secure method for dating a work such as Ezra and Nehemiah. A survey of textbooks and commentaries will reveal that a decision about this issue is invariably taken on the basis of other considerations, such as those we have just been discussing. For instance Rudolph, who accepts the whole of Ezra-Nehemiah as part of the work of the Chronicler, sees no reason to set a date later than 400 BC. By contrast, those who think that Ezra did not come to Jerusalem until 398 BC can hardly be expected to agree with him! Again, those who rate the evidence of 1 Esdras highly have to postulate several phases of composition, each with its own date, the latest coming down as far as the Maccabean period.

The very few pieces of possibly firmer evidence turn out on examination to be equally insecure. For instance, the reference to a high priest named Jaddua in Neh. 12.11 and 22 is frequently linked with the mention in Josephus, *Jewish Antiquities* 11.302ff., of a high priest of that name who held office at the time when Persian rule gave place to Hellenistic. Therefore, it is held, the books as a whole cannot be dated earlier than the Hellenistic period (late fourth century BC onwards). Others respond, however, that such lists may have been kept up to date after the books were completed, or that there was more than one Jaddua who acted as high priest, or that this passage as a whole is a later addition which cannot be used to date the main stages in the composition of these books. Clearly, it is better not to rely on such questionable details.

The best that we can hope to do here, therefore, is to follow through the implications for dating of the composition history just

proposed. The latest major part of the work, we have argued, is Ezra
1–6. As we shall see more fully later on, one of the major concerns of
the editor of this section was to justify the claim of the second temple
to be the legitimate successor of the Solomonic temple as Israel's sole
and central sanctuary. By a variety of means he stresses the lines of
continuity between the two in terms of site, structure, furnishings
and personnel. At the same time, he is careful to maintain a distance
between it and potentially rival claims from other groups within the
country at large (4.1-3). It then becomes attractive to suggest that a
need for such propaganda was especially acute at the time of the
founding of the Samaritan temple on Mount Gerizim early in the
Hellenistic period.

A date for Ezra 1–6 at this time would explain various other details
which may then be adduced as supporting evidence. The ascription
to Moses of the priestly and Levitical courses (Ezra 6.18), which is
not found in the Pentateuch, is likely to be later than the Chronicler's
ascription of them to David, and the borrowing of various elements
in chapter 3 from Chronicles (e.g. compare 3.7 with 1 Chron. 22.2-4
and 2 Chron. 2.8-16) points in the same direction.

Should this suggestion prove acceptable, then of course the other
major stage in the composition—the combining of the Ezra and the
Nehemiah material—must come earlier. On the traditional date for
Ezra's journey to Jerusalem (458 BC), the earliest date for this stage
would be the last recorded acts of Nehemiah in Neh. 13. These will
have to be dated late in the reign of Artaxerxes I, who died in 424 BC.
We then need to assume the passage of a certain amount of time in
order to allow the memories of the two reformers to merge to some
extent. They could, therefore, have been combined at any time after
about 400 BC. (Those who prefer the late date for Ezra will naturally
have to lower this date quite considerably.) We may thus ascribe
tentative dates of about 400 BC and 300 BC for the two major stages
in the composition of Ezra and Nehemiah.

Further Reading

The problems discussed in this chapter are so intertwined that it is difficult to categorize them satisfactorily under separate headings. However, the works which also include particular discussions of 1 Esdras are marked with a dagger (†):

R.L. Braun, 'Chronicles, Ezra, and Nehemiah: Theology and Literary History', in J.A. Emerton (ed.), *Studies in the Historical Books of the Old Testament* (SVT 30), Leiden: E.J. Brill, 1979, 52-64

†F.M. Cross, 'A Reconstruction of the Judean Restoration', *JBL* (1975), 4-18

S. Japhet, 'The Supposed Common Authorship of Chronicles and Ezra-Nehemiah Investigated Anew', *VT* 18 (1968), 330-71

†Mowinckel, *Studien 1*

Noth, *The Chronicler's History*

†K.-F. Pohlmann, *Studien zum dritten Esra* (FRLANT 104), Göttingen: Vandenhoeck & Ruprecht, 1970

S. Talmon, 'Ezra and Nehemiah', *IDBSup*, 317-28

†Torrey, *Ezra Studies*

†Williamson, *Israel*, 5-70

Williamson, 'The Composition of Ezra i-vi'

For a survey of older treatments of Ezra 4, see:

H.H. Rowley, 'Nehemiah's Mission and its Background', *Men of God*, London: Nelson, 1963, 211-45

Additional studies relevant to Neh. 8-10 include:

K. Baltzer, *The Covenant Formulary*, Oxford: Blackwell, 1971, 43-47

B.S. Childs, *Introduction to the Old Testament as Scripture*, London: SCM, 1979, 624-38

D.J. McCarthy, 'Covenant and Law in Chronicles-Nehemiah', *CBQ* 44 (1982), 25-44

Torrey, *Composition*, 29-34

On the Samaritans and their temple, see:

R.J. Bull, 'The Excavation of Tell er-Ras on Mt Gerizim', *BA* 31 (1968), 58-72

R.J. Coggins, *Samaritans and Jews. The Origins of Samaritanism Reconsidered*, Oxford: Blackwell, 1975

H.G. Kippenberg, *Garizim und Synagoge* (RVV 30), Berlin: de Gruyter, 1971

H.H. Rowley, 'Sanballat and the Samaritan Temple', *Men of God*, London: Nelson, 1963, 246-76

3

HISTORY

THE BOOKS of Ezra and Nehemiah are by far the most important sources for the history of Judah in the post-exilic period. Even though they leave large gaps in our knowledge, yet what can be learned from other sources both within and beyond the Bible is like rags by comparison. Not surprisingly, therefore, these books have been intensively scrutinized by historians and others in search of information which it was not the primary purpose of our authors and editors to convey. It is disappointing that in doing so they have not always paused to consider the importance and implications of first carefully analysing the literature as we have tried to do in the two preceding chapters. Some of the unfortunate effects of this failure will be illustrated below.

The range of historical problems raised by these books, and which are the subject of continuing debate, is considerable. It has been possible here to select only those which seem to me either to be most important or most prominent in modern scholarly discussion (the two are not always synonymous!).

A. The Political Status of the Province of Judah

For the past fifty years the political status of Judah within the Persian empire has been the subject of controversy. It is known from other sources that when the Persians inherited the Babylonian empire, they initially held it together as a single large province, known as a satrapy, and that later, during the reign of Darius I, it was divided into two—Babylon and 'Beyond the River' ('Trans-Euphrates' or Abar-nahara). It is also known that these satrapies were divided into smaller administrative units (provinces), usually with their own governor. There is no external evidence to indicate, however, whether Judah was a province of this kind from the beginning of Persian rule or only from some other later date.

In an influential article first published in 1934, A. Alt suggested that by the time the Babylonians eventually captured Jerusalem and put an end to the Davidic monarchy the country of Judah was already much reduced in size. In contrast with the Assyrian treatment of the northern kingdom of Israel, the Babylonians did not replace the upper classes whom they deported with new rulers brought in from outside. Instead, they simply annexed Judah to the already existing province of Samaria. This state of affairs, Alt maintained, continued unchanged when the Persians succeeded the Babylonians. Only when Nehemiah was appointed governor was Judah granted any degree of autonomy. This is why he stirred up such opposition especially in the north. Earlier apparent references to 'governors' of Judah mean no more than special commissioners; they do not indicate that Judah was an independent province.

Alt's article persuaded many subsequent scholars, and his view has recently been defended anew by McEvenue against those who have opposed it. (Stern has also appealed to it to explain changes in the style of official seal impressions at about this time, but this does not amount to independent evidence in its favour.) Despite its attractive features, however, it has been criticized on several grounds. Morton Smith, for instance, has rightly emphasized that Alt's case is hypothetical, based at best on circumstantial evidence. Without illustrating this in detail, it is perhaps sufficient to observe that we are nowhere told that Judah was annexed to Samaria, and indeed Nebuchadnezzar's appointment of Gedaliah as governor after the fall of Jerusalem (2 Kgs 25.23) might be thought to point in the opposite direction. It should also be noted that we are not told of Nehemiah's appointment as governor either (though that is clearly what he was), so that arguments from silence are precarious supports for either side in the debate.

Second, and tellingly, Smith has accused Alt of not giving adequate weight to Neh. 5.14-15, where Nehemiah boasts that he has not burdened the people in the way that 'the earlier governors who came before me' did. Smith contends that 'the earlier governors' can hardly be special commissioners or governors of Samaria since Nehemiah's whole case would fail if like is not being compared with like.

Widengren too has dissented from Alt's conclusions, largely on linguistic grounds. The terms for 'province' and 'governor' are certainly used in some places in their technical senses, and though it is admitted by all that they are used flexibly elsewhere in the Old Testament, Alt's case becomes progressively weaker the larger the accumulation of such exceptional cases becomes. To these considerations we may add the question why, if Judah was not an independent province with Jerusalem as its capital, the various official enquiries in Ezra 4 and 5 were necessary at all: presumably on Alt's view the governor of Samaria should have had authority to act within his own province, while Tattenai in Ezra 5 should have approached him, and not the Jews, for an explanation of what was going on. On the whole, it seems preferable to take Ezra 5.14 at its face value and to accept that Sheshbazzar was the first to be appointed governor by the Persians, and to deduce from this that they administered Judah as a separate province within the Satrapy of Beyond the River. The relative silence of Ezra-Nehemiah about the political status of prominent figures in the restoration period has been explained by Japhet on the basis of the editor's ideology (on which see Chapter 4 below).

Further Reading

There are several up-to-date histories of the Achaemenid (Persian) empire which include discussion of the system of satrapies:

> J.M. Cook, *The Persian Empire*, London: Dent, 1983, especially
> chs. viii and xvi
> R.N. Frye, *The History of Ancient Iran*, Munich: Beck, 1984,
> especially pp. 106-20
> I. Gershevitch (ed.), *The Cambridge History of Iran, vol. 2: The
> Median and Achaemenian Periods*, Cambridge: University
> Press, 1985, especially chs. 5 and 10

Alt's article, originally published in 1934, is now most conveniently available in:

> A. Alt, 'Die Rolle Samarias bei der Entstehung des Judentums',
> *Kleine Schriften* II, Munich: Beck, 1953, 316-37

Amongst those who have adopted and developed his position, we may note especially:

> S. McEvenue, 'The Political Structure in Judah from Cyrus to
> Nehemiah', *CBQ* 43 (1981), 353-64
> E. Stern, *Material Culture of the Land of the Bible in the Persian

Period 538-332 B.C., Warminster: Aris and Phillips, 1982, ch. 7 (This book also deserves mention as an authoritative and up-to-date mine of information on many important background topics for the study of Ezra and Nehemiah; note especially ch. 9 on the geographical history of Palestine in this period and the history of settlement.)

Alt's view has been contested principally by:

M. Smith, *Palestinian Parties and Politics that Shaped the Old Testament*, New York and London: Columbia University Press, 1971, especially the Appendix (pp. 193-201), 'Alt's Account of the Samaritans'

G. Widengren, 'The Persian Period', in J.H. Hayes and J.M. Miller (eds.), *Israelite and Judaean History*, London: SCM, 1977, 489-538 (especially 509-11); this chapter generally supplies a concise and independent survey of most of the historical problems raised by Ezra and Nehemiah

N. Avigad, *Bullae and Seals from a Post-Exilic Judean Archive* (Qedem 4), Jerusalem: Institute of Archaeology, The Hebrew University, 1976. Avigad here published (*inter alia*) a bulla and a seal which probably carry the name and title of a governor of Judah; however, it cannot be claimed as certain that they are to be dated earlier than Nehemiah

S. Japhet, 'Sheshbazzar and Zerubbabel', *ZAW* 94 (1982), 66-98

B. The Building of the Second Temple

Several historical problems arise with regard to the account in Ezra 1-6 of the building of the second temple, but we can here deal with only two: (1) What was the course of events prior to the successful building? (2) What happened to Zerubbabel?

The first question might appear to be simply answered (as some scholars have tried to do) by a 'flat' reading of the present text: very soon after the united return of Jews from Babylon in the first or second year of Cyrus (Ezra 1-2), the exiles gathered at Jerusalem to rededicate the altar (Ezra 3.1-6). A year or two later, a start was made on the building under the direction of Zerubbabel and Jeshua (Ezra 3.7-13), but this was soon stopped by outside interference (4.1-4). Work only resumed some seventeen years later, in the second year of Darius, under the influence of the prophets Haggai and Zechariah (Ezra 5-6).

In support of this outline, its defenders explain away various difficulties which others have raised. For instance, how can it be reconciled with the statement of Ezra 5.16 that Sheshbazzar, not Zerubbabel, laid the foundations of the new temple? Answer: either identify Sheshbazzar with Zerubbabel (following Josephus) or, preferably, explain that while Zerubbabel was actually responsible for the foundation-laying, the Jews in Ezra 5 attributed the work to Sheshbazzar because it would have been his name that was recorded in the Persian archives (cf. 1.8). Zerubbabel was simply acting under his authority.

Again, how can the picture presented be squared with the impression gained from the book of Haggai that the work begun in 520 BC (the second year of Darius) was a fresh undertaking rather than the continuation of an interrupted work? Answer: after a gap of nearly twenty years, little evidence would remain of the first unsuccessful undertaking. Furthermore, 'to found' in Hag. 2.18 need not imply a completely fresh start, for elsewhere it is used with some such meaning as 'to restore'; cf. 2 Chron. 24.27

The major alternative approach seeks to take these difficulties more seriously and to emphasize the gaps which our sources leave. For instance, not one of our primary sources (see the discussion in Chapter 1 above) gives any indication of when the return from Babylon took place, nor even whether it all took place at once. The conservative view is merely an assumption based upon the fact that Ezra 2 follows Ezra 1. Furthermore, as we have seen, the date in 3.1 (which in any case does not mention a year) is simply taken over from Neh. 7.73 and is therefore devoid of any independent value. The consensus of opinion amongst those who take this approach is that 3.1–4.3 is a source *parallel with* the Aramaic equivalent in Ezra 5–6. Zerubbabel built the temple early in the reign of Darius: whatever unspecified measures Sheshbazzar may have taken previously are irrelevant.

It should be clear by now that we ought to have a certain sympathy with this second approach; but does it go far enough? What is the evidence that 3.1–4.3 is a 'source' at all? It does not have the characteristics of any of the other sources with which the editor of Ezra 1–6 was working, but it has certain other special features to which justice has not yet been done.

The most important point to notice is that no source was needed for our author to compose most of this passage: it can practically all be deduced from other material which we know was available to him, once we grant that his purpose was to draw attention to parallels with the building of the first temple. As examples of this dependence, we may cite the following, to which more could be added: for 3.1, cf. Neh. 7.73–8.1; for 3.7, cf. 1 Chron. 22.2-4 and 2 Chron. 2.8-16; for the date in 3.8, cf. 2 Chron. 3.2; for the rest of 3.8, cf. 1 Chron. 23.4; for Zerubbabel's initiative in laying the foundation (3.10), cf. Zech. 4.9; for 3.10-11, see 2 Chron. 5.11ff. and 7.6; for 3.12-13 see Hag. 2.3; and so on! On the basis of all this evidence, it may be suggested that the editor's aim was not to give an historical account at this point at all; that was to follow with the inclusion of first-hand sources in Ezra 5–6. Rather, he has here prefaced that account with a highly stylized presentation, a major part of whose purpose was to demonstrate the legitimacy of the second temple as successor to the first. At the same time he emphasized the Jews' eagerness to build and their frustration because of external interference.

If this approach is justified, then it may be worth making the further suggestion that Ezra 4.4-5 should be identified as what Talmon has termed a 'summary notation'. The purpose of this device is not to describe a new step in the historical development, but rather to summarize the whole of the previous section. According to this view, the reference to the people of the land making the Jews afraid to build will recapitulate 3.3, and 4.5 will imply that no work at all was done on the temple until the start of Darius's reign. In other words, 4.4-5 will be the narrator's way of explaining that 3.1-6 refers to an altar dedication in the reign of Cyrus, but that for fear of the 'peoples of the land' no building was undertaken at that time. 3.7–4.3 describes the start of the work in the time of Darius and so introduces the more matter-of-fact account of chs. 5–6. Whilst this suggestion leaves several historical questions unanswered, it at least has the merit of trying to come to terms with the constraints which our much later editor must have faced in view of the relative paucity of the sources at his disposal.

The other main question relating to this period concerns the role and fate of Zerubbabel. He was a member of the Davidic family (1 Chron. 3.19). Moreover, it is clear from the contemporary Hag. 1.12-15; 2.20-23 and Zech. 4.6-10 (to go no further) that he was a prominent leader when the building began and that certain circles vested political messianic hopes in him. As far as it goes, this fits well with Ezra 5.1-2.

A persistent minority of scholars, however, has made considerable play of the observation that no mention is made of Zerubbabel at the completion and dedication of the temple in Ezra 6.13-22. They also suggest that his name may have been deleted from Zech. 6.9-15. Now, since we know from Darius's own account in his Behistun inscription that he spent much of the opening years of his reign crushing rebellions all over his empire and dealing severely with a rash of local pretenders, it has been possible to put two and two together and to propose that Zerubbabel was removed from office—if not executed—by the Persians because of supposed messianic pretensions.

Here is a good example of an historical reconstruction (often repeated in text-books) which takes little account of sober literary analysis. As we have seen, the editor of Ezra 1-6 wrote long after the events he describes and has no information beyond the official documents which he used as his sources. That arguments from silence are thus more than usually dangerous is clear from the fact that he is unable to include any description of the actual building of the temple at all! His account of the dedication of the temple at the end of Ezra 6 appears to be no more than a reflection on the dedication of the first temple (1 Kgs 8) in the light of the cultic practices of his own day. Silence about Zerubbabel's involvement need thus be no more significant than his comparable silence about Jeshua the high priest—although no one has accused him of involvement in any conspiracy. Again, Darius makes no mention of any such revolt in his Behistun inscription, where it might have been expected, and it is possible to argue on the basis of Zech. 4.9 that Zerubbabel indeed saw the completion of the building. Finally, it is strange that no mention is made of insurrection either in Tattenai's inquiry (Ezra 5.6-17) or in Darius's reply (6.1-12)—rather the reverse (6.7)! We have no choice, therefore, but to conclude that we do not know what happened to Zerubbabel; we must respect the absence of source material and rest content with ignorance about this as about many other related matters.

Further Reading

Translations of the Behistun Inscription are available in R.G. Kent, *Old Persian: Grammar; Texts; Lexicon* (2nd edn, AOS 33), New Haven: American Oriental Society, 1953, pp. 116-34, and Frye, *History of Ancient Iran*, Appendix 2. For other topics discussed in this section, see:

P.R. Ackroyd, *Exile and Restoration*, London: SCM, 1968, 38-52

K.-M. Beyse, *Serubbabel und die Königserwartungen der Propheten Haggai und Sacharja*, Stuttgart: Calwer Verlag, 1972

R.J. Coggins, *Haggai, Zechariah, Malachi* (OT Guides), Sheffield: JSOT Press, 1987, ch. 1

A. Gelston, 'The Foundations of the Second Temple', *VT* 16 (1966), 232-35

L. Waterman, 'The Camouflaged Purge of Three Messianic Conspirators', *JNES* 13 (1954), 73-78

J.S. Wright, *The Building of the Second Temple*, London: Tyndale Press, 1958

C. The Chronological Order of Ezra and Nehemiah

1. *Orientation*

We come now to what is undoubtedly the most frequently discussed historical problem raised by the books of Ezra and Nehemiah. Indeed, it is not impossible that hard-pressed students with deadlines to meet for the submission of their essays may be tempted to turn for guidance straight to this section. It is important, therefore, to realize that this topic cannot be properly understood in isolation from a literary analysis such as is attempted in the first two chapters of this book. In particular, the following points need to be borne in mind: the sources which give us reliable information about Ezra and Nehemiah were originally written in complete independence of each other, and without any 'cross-references'. Only Ezra 7-10 and Neh. 8 tell us about Ezra, and we have favoured the view that the substance of Neh. 8 originally stood in the Ezra source between Ezra 8 and 9. The whole of Ezra's recorded ministry thus lasted just one year. We have also argued that the intertwining of the material about Ezra and Nehemiah was one of the first steps in the composition of the books as a whole, but we have noted the opinion of many other scholars that it was one of the last, and may even have been initially the result of a scribal mistake.

Two other preliminary points also deserve mention. First, the Artaxerxes of the Nehemiah memoir is generally agreed to be Artaxerxes I. The date of Nehemiah's journey to Jerusalem will thus be 445 BC. Although a few voices have been raised against this consensus, their arguments are not at all convincing and they have rightly been rejected by the overwhelming majority. It hardly seems necessary to discuss the matter here, and so the usual date for Nehemiah will be assumed throughout.

Second, we shall also assume that the Ezra memoir gives us reliable information about Ezra's activities. Obviously, if Ezra did not exist (Torrey), no problem arises. Similarly, if most of the material relating to him is the Chronicler's midrash on the Artaxerxes edict (see Chapter 1 §B above), many of the points in the debate lose their force, though the basic question would remain. However, in order to deal fully with the problem, we shall have to treat the account at face value.

The point at issue, therefore, boils down to the date of Ezra's journey to Jerusalem. There are three main views, with distinguished scholars championing each. According to Ezra 7.7-8, Ezra travelled in the seventh year of Artaxerxes. At first glance, the Biblical text implies that this was Artaxerxes I, and that this date is therefore 458 BC, thirteen years before Nehemiah. This date was unquestioned until 1889, and it has never lacked support. Indeed, recent years have seen an increasing number defending it in preference to the alternatives which we shall note below.

The major alternative is to date Ezra in the seventh year of Artaxerxes II, i.e. 398 BC, well after Nehemiah. Since, as we have seen, the Ezra material was initially an independent source, this is not so radical a proposal as it might first appear. It involves no textual emendation of Ezra 7 and it is believed to remove a number of difficulties which confront the traditional date.

The third view proposes that Ezra came to Jerusalem not in the seventh, but in the thirty-seventh year of Artaxerxes I, i.e. 428 BC. (Rudolph suggests a slightly earlier date during the interval between Nehemiah's first and second term as governor, i.e. 432 BC at the earliest.) The most easily accessible presentation of this view in English is that of John Bright in his influential *History of Israel*. Upholders of this approach might be accused of trying to keep their cake and eat it: they allow themselves to do full justice to the difficulties in putting Ezra first, but they try also to avoid the problems raised by dating him as late as 398 BC. They also enjoy the advantage of being able to exploit the similarities between Ezra's reforms and those of Nehemiah's second term (Neh. 13).

2. *Elimination of the* 428 BC *option*

Despite its attractiveness, the third view confronts various weighty objections and matters may be clearer if we eliminate it first.

(a) The theory demands a totally unsupported conjectural emendation of the text of Ezra 7.7-8, a conjecture not strengthened by the fact that it has to be made twice (once in each verse). There is nothing in the Hebrew text at this point to suggest that it has suffered corruption nor any adequate explanation of how and why the error arose. (The fact that in Hebrew the words for 'thirty' and 'three' both start with the letter *š* is hardly sufficient, and in any case does not explain v. 8 where the wording is slightly different, and so would have to have been deliberately changed.) The theory thus suffers from the outset the drawback of special pleading, and as a point of method it should not be accepted unless all else fails.

(b) If Ezra came after Nehemiah, there is no good reason why 428 BC should be preferred to 398 BC. This was the burden of a very thorough study of the matter by Emerton, to which it is disappointing that Bright has not responded fully in the later editions of his *History*. It is perhaps unnecessary to repeat all the arguments here, but we may cite one as an example where Emerton's hand can now in fact be strengthened. In Ezra 10.6, Ezra withdraws to the temple chamber of one Jehohanan, son of Eliashib. It is believed by many on the basis of the Elephantine Papyri that he was the high priest in 398 BC. However, in his *Jewish Antiquities* 11.297-301, Josephus tells a story about how a high priest Johanan murdered his brother in the temple. Thus Bright is able to challenge: would Ezra have consorted with a murderer, as proponents of the 398 BC date have to believe? Emerton replied that perhaps Ezra regarded the killing as 'an act of self-defence against an attack by a godless would-be usurper'. In fact, however, as I have sought to argue in detail on quite other grounds, Josephus's story almost certainly comes from the much later reign of Artaxerxes III and is therefore of no relevance whatever to the date of Ezra.

(c) If Ezra and Nehemiah were working on similar reforms at the same time the difficulty of the fact that they apparently ignore each other completely becomes more acute. It is true that, for instance, Haggai and Zechariah do not refer to each other, but they are prophets with a largely spoken ministry. Ezra and Nehemiah were implementing reforms in the course of which their paths would have had to cross.

The general arguments for putting Ezra after Nehemiah (on which both the 428 BC and the 398 BC theories depend) will be examined below. It seems best, in view of the objections listed, to eliminate the 428 BC option from further consideration.

3. *Arguments from Achaemenid Policy*

Turning now to the substance of the debate, we find that the arguments break down into three major categories. The first group seek to relate Ezra's mission to the broader issue of Persian imperial policy.

(a) In favour of the traditional date, it can be observed that the period of 459-448 BC was a turbulent one in the west. It started with a revolt against Persian rule in Egypt and this was immediately followed by a rebellion led by a certain Megabyzos, who attracted widespread support in the satrapy of Beyond the River. It is thus reasonable to suppose that the Persians would have welcomed a sympathetic leader in Judah.

Similarly, as has been argued especially by Cazelles, the empire passed through troubled times at the turn of the century. In 401 BC Egypt again rebelled, and this time she regained her independence. Artaxerxes II was then faced with several years of revolt led by his brother Cyrus.

None of our sources, Biblical or otherwise, makes any direct connection between these events and Ezra's mission, and the two sets of circumstances seem to cancel each other out. If we knew Ezra's date, we might hazard a guess as to the Persians' ulterior motives in sending him to Jerusalem, but conversely a knowledge of their policy cannot help us to fix that date in the first place.

(b) A further argument of this sort relates to the 'Passover Papyrus' (*AP*, no. 21) from Elephantine, an Egyptian military outpost on the border between Egypt and Ethiopia which included a sizeable Jewish colony. Although the papyrus is badly damaged, the usual understanding of it may be accepted, namely that it represents an attempt by the Persian authorities to enforce the laws relating to the Feast of Unleavened Bread and Passover on the Jewish colony there. It is dated in 419 BC. Bright in particular has urged that Ezra's mission must have already taken place before that because of the unlikelihood that 'Jewish practice was being regulated in a far corner of Egypt—and perhaps via Jerusalem—before this had been done in Jerusalem itself'.

Bright's interpretation is a possible one—but not the only one. It is not certain, for instance, that Ezra's mission was a total innovation; it may have been a reaffirmation of existing policy, an attempt to restore a situation that had lapsed. Again, Porten has suggested that the Papyrus may be a 'reaffirmation of the Jews' right to observe the Passover in the face of Egyptian antagonism'. After all, the Papyrus refers to only one aspect of the Law rather than to the Law as a whole. We may conclude that the Passover Papyrus cannot support a late date for Ezra. One interpretation of it might favour an early date, but this is by no means certain. It is thus best not used as evidence either way.

(c) Finally, Kellermann has maintained that the encouragement of local law was a characteristic of the first rather than the second half of Achaemenid rule; he therefore thinks that Ezra should be dated in the reign of Artaxerxes I as a late example of this early Achaemenid policy.

This line of argument too is very far from decisive. On the one hand, on the basis of the evidence which Kellermann himself presents, it is difficult to put a specific date on this presumed change in Achaemenid policy. On the other hand, such considerations do not seem to rule out a late date for Ezra: if the Jews had early been granted a measure of religious freedom, there is no good reason why later kings should not have continued this policy if it was in their interests to do so.

We may therefore conclude this section by affirming that the date of Ezra will have to be determined on the basis of Biblical evidence alone.

4. *Arguments from Details in the Biblical Text*
The second group of arguments relating to the date of Ezra focuses on a large number of individual details which it is thought can be most easily explained on the assumption that Ezra came later than Nehemiah. Those who favour the traditional date for Ezra, by contrast, seek to explain away the difficulties which have been raised. There are quite a number of these points, and it will not be possible to deal with them all here. Some, it is now generally agreed, are so weak as to be of no value in the debate: if Ezra came after Nehemiah, these verses might be explained in the manner suggested, but they carry no weight in deciding the issue in the first place.

In the following summary, we shall first give the main arguments of those who favour a late date for Ezra and then the conservative response. It is naturally up to the reader to decide in each case which side seems the stronger and whether any are decisive either way.

(a) In his prayer in Ezra 9, Ezra gives thanks to God for, amongst other things, having given us 'a wall in Judah and Jerusalem'. It has thus been argued that when Ezra came to Jerusalem, he found a wall already built, thus presupposing the work of Nehemiah.

In response to this it may be observed that in all probability the word 'wall' is here being used metaphorically (cf. Ps. 80.12): some of the other items for which Ezra gives thanks are clearly to be understood so, and in this case the probability is strengthened by the qualification 'in Judah and Jerusalem', which would, to say the least, be a curious way of referring to the city wall. In addition, we should note that the Hebrew word used here (*gādēr*) is not the common one for a city wall (*ḥômāh*): it usually refers to a wall or fence around a vineyard or along a road. (Was Ezra thinking of the people under the traditional metaphor of Israel as God's vineyard, Isa. 5.1-7?) Several modern English translations thus prefer to render the word 'protection'.

(b) It seems that Jerusalem was a well populated city in Ezra's time (cf. Ezra 10.1) but not in Nehemiah's time, since Nehemiah had to take steps to move people in to inhabit it (Neh. 7.4-5; 11.1-2). This is more easily understood if Ezra followed Nehemiah.

Several points can be made in replying to this. (i) Ezra 10.1 does not say that the crowd who gathered round Ezra comprised only residents of Jerusalem. (ii) A thinly populated city can still produce a large crowd if a large proportion of the people come together in one place. (iii) According to Ezra 4.23, Jerusalem had suffered a disaster shortly before Nehemiah's time (see also Neh. 1.3). It would thus not be surprising if its population had been reduced.

(c) In Neh. 13.13 Nehemiah establishes a committee which Ezra appears to have found in being when he arrived in Jerusalem (Ezra 8.33).

This is by no means the only interpretation of the data. (i) The constitution of the committee is quite different in each case—two priests and two Levites in Ezra; a priest, a scribe, a Levite and a layman in Nehemiah. So is it the same committee in each case? (ii) Similarly, their functions are not identical. In Ezra the subject is the temple treasures whereas in Nehemiah it is the collection and distribution of tithes. (iii) There is nothing in Ezra 8.33 to suggest that we are dealing with a standing committee. It could just as well be an *ad hoc* representative group of temple officials, as Ezra 8.29

perhaps implies. (iv) Alternatively, it is not certain that Nehemiah is setting up a committee for the first time. It is possible that when he revived the practice of tithing he also revived the system for administering it equitably.

(d) Linked with the previous point is the case of Meremoth son of Uriah the priest. The following are the relevant data: the first member of the 'committee' to whom Ezra handed over the temple treasures in Ezra 8.33 was 'Meremoth the son of Uriah, the priest'. At Neh. 3.4 and 21, Meremoth son of Uriah, son of Hakkoz, is listed as an energetic wall-builder in Nehemiah's day. Though he is not called a priest, the others in this section of the list are either Levites or priests. The reference to Hakkoz further directs attention to Ezra 2.61 where the priestly family of Hakkoz was unable to prove its descent at the time of the return from Babylon.

Some believe that these data favour the priority of Nehemiah: in Nehemiah's time the family still lived under a cloud, but Meremoth's outstanding efforts on the wall-building led to their reinstatement.

There are, however, other reasonable ways of explaining the situation:

(i) Since both the names Meremoth and Uriah are common, no identification need be made (so Kellermann).

(ii) Koch argues for Meremoth's demotion rather than promotion, and so retains the traditional order. In Ezra 8.33 Meremoth appears as the supreme priest, while in Neh. 3 he is not explicitly called a priest at all. 'It seems as if Ezra acknowledged Meremoth at the time of the arrival in Jerusalem, but deposed him shortly afterward while carrying out his investigation in Jerusalem by means of the law he had brought with him.' However, as no Meremoth is mentioned in the list of Ezra 10 (those involved in mixed marriages), this suggestion of Koch seems somewhat speculative.

(iii) On the assumption that the same man is referred to in both Ezra 8 and Neh. 3, the traditional order could nevertheless be correct. As most scholars agree, he is likely to be a priest in Neh. 3, for there are other priests listed there who are not specifically so designated. He could well have been a temple treasurer when Ezra returned in 458 BC (but not the high priest: he is not listed as such in Neh. 12) and still easily have been able to act as a section-leader in the wall-building thirteen years later. This view needs to assume only that his family's 'descent' had been cleared up during the fifty or more years prior to Ezra's mission.

(e) Some have found especially compelling the fact that Nehemiah is listed before Ezra in Neh. 12.26. Clines, p. 20, neatly counters this, however, by asking, 'By what means, may we suppose, has the correct order of Nehemiah-Ezra been preserved here when it has been systematically confused (on this view) by the Chronicler everywhere else?' In fact, it is probable that this whole passage is a late addition to the work: verse 26 divides the period of return and restoration into two—'the days of Joiakim', which refers to the generation of the return, and 'the days of Nehemiah . . . and Ezra', referring to their united reform. This will be as much a reflection on the literary tradition as on historical memory; as such it is most revealing theologically, as we shall see in Chapter 4, but it does not make for good historical evidence.

(f) Rather than prolonging this list unduly, we shall come now to what is potentially the strongest argument of this sort in favour of a late date for Ezra. During his handling of the mixed marriages affair, Ezra at one stage 'departed from in front of the house of God and withdrew to the chamber of Jehohanan the son of Eliashib, and he spent the night there . . .' (Ezra 10.6). Now, we know that the high priest when Nehemiah came to Jerusalem was called Eliashib (cf. Neh. 3.1) and we know too that later on there was a high priest called Johanan (cf. Neh. 12.22; Johanan and Jehohanan are simply variant forms of the same name). This latter fact is independently confirmed by the Elephantine papyri, where there is a reference to a Jehohanan who was high priest in Jerusalem towards the end of the fifth century BC. If this is the Jehohanan of Ezra 10.6, then it would seem clear that Ezra should be dated after Nehemiah. Indeed, several scholars are willing to rest more or less the whole of their case on this argument.

Attractive as this case may appear, we should be clear in our minds both that it glosses over certain difficulties and that alternative explanations are possible. First, although this is not absolutely necessary, the argument is generally taken a step further by advocates of the reverse order. It is assumed from Neh. 12.22 that Johanan was in fact Eliashib's grandson. Furthermore, since in Neh. 12.10-11 the grandson of Eliashib is called Jonathan, it is suggested that Jonathan there is a scribal error for Johanan. Finally, in order to tie all the verses together, 'son' in our verse (Ezra 10.6) as well as at Neh. 12.23 is said to mean 'grandson'.

None of these points is securely based, however. There is no evidence for the proposed alteration in Neh. 12.10-11 (where in fact the name Jonathan occurs twice). Similarly, although 'son' can sometimes have the more general meaning of 'descendant', this is usually in contexts where there is good reason for such terminology, as with the descendant of the founder of a dynasty. Since such reasons are lacking here, as both Mowinckel and Porter have independently pointed out, Johanan should be regarded as indeed the son of Eliashib.

Despite these objections, it is still perfectly reasonable to claim that the Johanan of Ezra 10.6 is the high priest of later times. However, he is not given the title which we should expect, and this opens the way for us to consider alternative explanations:

(i) Still maintaining the same identities, it would be possible for Johanan to have been a young man in 458 BC and to have become high priest by the end of the century. The fact that he had a room in the temple does not necessarily mean that he was the high priest, nor is it convincing to argue, as some have, that Ezra could have withdrawn only to the high priest's chambers.

(ii) Another possibility is that by the writer's time that particular room was known under this name because of its former association with a famous high priest. The use of the name in Ezra 10.6 must then be regarded as a common-enough type of anachronism.

(iii) We move to consider next a suggestion which proposes a different set of identifications but which still maintains that the high-priestly family is referred to in Ezra 10.6. There is a strong probability that we do not know the names of all the high priests of the Persian period; if we do, several of them must have lived long and given birth to their eldest sons at an unusually advanced age! In an influential article, F.M. Cross has sought to fill in the gaps in the list on the assumption that the high priest's family adopted the practice of papponymy (naming a child after his grandfather). Other evidence makes this a likely assumption. In that case, there may have been an Eliashib and Johanan *before* the Eliashib of Nehemiah's day and thus contemporary with a traditionally dated Ezra.

Cross's presentation is certainly open to criticism, as Widengren, pp. 506-509, has pointed out, on the grounds that it is 'based on so many uncertainties and reconstructions, as well as one fundamental mistake' (namely Cross's assertion that Eliashib was the brother, rather than the son, of Joiakim; cf. Neh. 12.10). Nevertheless, Cross's

starting point—the fact that the names of some high priests are lost—
is probably correct. In that case it remains possible that there was an
earlier high priest Johanan, son of Eliashib.

(iv) A final possibility is that the reference in Ezra 10.6 is not to the
high-priestly family at all. After all, both names were extremely
common at the time, several men called Eliashib or Johanan being
known from other lists of this period. In particular, it is of interest to
observe that at Neh. 13.4 there is reference to an 'Eliashib the priest
who was appointed over the chambers of the house of our God'. This
definition seems intended to identify Eliashib and therefore, contrary
to the opinion of several commentators, it is presumably meant to
distinguish him from Eliashib the high priest. We should not expect
the high priest to function as a caretaker. The association of this
Eliashib with a temple chamber links back to Ezra 10.6, for the same
word for 'chamber' is used in both verses. Perhaps, therefore, the
reference in Ezra 10.6 is to this family rather than the high priest's. If
so, Ezra could still be dated after Nehemiah if the Eliashib in both
verses is the same. On the other hand, in view of the evidence that
papponymy was widely practised at the time, the Eliashib of Ezra
10.6 could equally well be the grandfather of the one in Neh. 13.4,
thus allowing the early date for Ezra.

I have purposely dealt with Ezra 10.6 in some detail, both because
it is generally regarded as one of the strongest arguments for dating
Ezra after Nehemiah and because it well illustrates how difficult it is
to arrive at a firm decision on the matter. Different scholars evaluate
the evidence differently, and it is for each reader to make up his or
her own mind. Some other arguments of this nature are best treated
in our final section immediately below, and others (generally agreed
to be weaker) will be found in the works listed at the end. For what it
is worth, my own opinion is that neither on their own nor
cumulatively do these arguments from individual texts *demand* that
Ezra be dated after Nehemiah, although most are compatible with
that suggestion. In that case, we shall have to look for other grounds
on which to come to a decision.

5. *A broader consideration of the Biblical evidence*
Since it is uncomfortable to sit on a fence for too long, it is high time
that I jump off and state clearly what most readers will have already
guessed, namely that I favour an early (458 BC) date for Ezra's
journey to Jerusalem. My reasons will become clear in the considera-

tions advanced in this section. It is therefore worth emphasizing at the outset that proof in this matter is unobtainable, and so it must be left to others to judge whether justice is being done to alternative points of view.

(a) The history of composition proposed in Chapter 2 suggests that considerable weight should be given to the testimony of the present text that Ezra came to Jerusalem in the seventh year of Artaxerxes I. We have argued that the combining of the narratives about Ezra and Nehemiah was the first step towards the composition of the books as a whole. We are therefore not faced with a situation where historical memory could have become badly distorted by the passage of a lengthy interval in time; if Ezra came as late as 398 BC, we are coming perilously close to the period of our editor. One can understand that his desire to treat the work of the two reformers as a united act of restoration under God's hand could have led the memory of them to merge to some extent, but is it credible that he should have been mistaken on so fundamental a matter as which king commissioned Ezra? After all, if Ezra travelled in the reign of Artaxerxes II, it is quite likely that it would have been within the lifetime of some of the editor's contemporaries.

(b) Although neither reformer refers directly to the work of the other, it is possible to suggest that some of Nehemiah's actions and those of his contemporaries presuppose the ministry of Ezra rather than vice versa. (It is worth mentioning here that I cannot see the force of the counter-proposal that Ezra could not have contemplated undertaking his reforms before Nehemiah had built the wall. Historically speaking, the two activities are not closely related and the kind of arguments which suggest they are would be unlikely to have entered Artaxerxes' head when he dispatched Ezra on his mission.)

We shall argue later that Ezra's greatest achievement was not to introduce a new law to Judah, but to establish new guidelines for its application. With Israel's loss of national sovereignty, many of the laws in the Pentateuch could no longer be literally or directly obeyed. It seems, therefore, as though there was a danger of them becoming a dead letter to many in the community. From the record of Ezra's ministry as we have it, he was responsible for initiating techniques of interpretation, techniques which have been employed in one way or another ever since, of bringing originally separate laws into relationship with one another in order to give them a new lease of life, and of seeking out the spirit, rather than the letter, of the law as a whole. One prominent example of this is the Scriptural rationale for the condemnation of mixed marriages in Ezra 9.1-2. This condemnation is repeated, however, by Nehemiah in Neh. 13.25 with the citation of just one of the laws on which Ezra's hermeneutic is based. Taken on its own, the law cited by Nehemiah was not fully appropriate to the case in hand. It had only become to be regarded so because of the way in which Ezra interpreted it.

A similar point can be made about the approach to the law which was embodied in the community pledge of Neh. 10.29-39. We saw in Chapter 1 that this pledge was closely related in time to Nehemiah's second term as governor. Once again, however, it seems to presuppose that approach to the law which Ezra first introduced.

(c) The mention of mixed marriages brings us to a point which has been frequently advanced as a strong argument for dating Ezra after Nehemiah. In Neh. 13.23-27 Nehemiah deals piecemeal and with characteristic vigour with some isolated instances of this abuse. His approach, it is said, was unsuccessful and so Ezra was later obliged to deal with the issue more systematically. (We may note here in passing that in fact, if Josephus is to be believed, neither reformer succeeded in eradicating the practice of mixed marriages, for they are said to have continued throughout the subsequent century.)

To me, the passages in question make much better sense if this argument is turned on its head! It is not just that Nehemiah dealt with a few cases: it is rather that they were extremely localized, reference being made only to 'women of Ashdod, of Ammon and of Moab' (Neh. 13.23). Ashdod here is understandable, as it had a land border with Judah on the west. Other such areas, notably Samaria to the north, which we might have expected to find here, are strangely absent (except for the one case of 13.28). In the next verse, Nehemiah is incensed that some of the children of these marriages spoke Ashdodite, but no mention is made of Ammonite and Moabite. When it is further realized that 'Ammon and Moab' are tacked on in the Hebrew text without the use of the conjunction 'and' (a construction as curious in Hebrew as it would be in English), it becomes probable, as others have also suggested, that 'Ammon and Moab' are really only added as a legal explanation of the status of Ashdod, for earlier in the chapter we have been reminded of the Deuteronomic law that 'an Ammonite and a Moabite should not enter into the assembly of God for ever' (Neh. 13.1).

Even without this last point, it is clear that Nehemiah was not confronted by a problem that was rife throughout Judaean society, but one which was localized to one, or at most two, of its border areas. His reaction is inexplicable if the situation was as it appears to have been before Ezra's arrival. Why should he have been so taken aback at stumbling across particular examples of what was a widespread practice? And why did he deal with these cases, but not the others? It makes much better sense to suppose that Ezra had already dealt with the problem as a whole, and that Nehemiah was merely dealing with isolated cases of its resurgence—nipping them in the bud before they gained a wider foothold.

(d) A small, but related, point concerns the degree of support which Ezra received in his handling of this affair. Nehemiah, it appears, had the knack of antagonizing those with whom he disagreed, and we may deduce from his treatment of Tobiah (Neh. 13.4-8) and Sanballat's son-in-law (13.28) that he would not have endeared the whole population (least of all the priests) to a policy of rigorous separation. In that case, it would be hard to explain the widespread support which Ezra found when he tackled the issue if this followed Nehemiah. It looks, rather, as though the agreement which his measures received came before attitudes towards the matter had hardened.

(e) Finally, because in some areas the work of the two reformers overlapped, it is frequently assumed that one or other of them must have failed. It is possible to exaggerate this assumption, but as far as it goes it surely points if anything to the priority of Ezra. As we shall see below, Ezra did not succeed in fulfilling all the terms of Artaxerxes' commission, and historically speaking his work seems to come to an abrupt end. (This does not imply, however, that he was in any way involved in the abortive attempt to build the walls as reported out of chronological order at Ezra 4.7-23.) Nehemiah, on the other hand, achieved all that he set out to do, and a good deal more besides. Perhaps more importantly, Nehemiah enjoyed much greater authority than Ezra by virtue of his appointment as governor. It would then be strange if Ezra came later without such authority in order to complete what Nehemiah had failed to achieve.

For these reasons amongst others, it seems to me best to date Ezra's journey to Jerusalem in 458 BC.

Further Reading

The date of Ezra has been so frequently debated that a full listing of the literature would serve little purpose. It is worth remembering, however, that some attention is paid to it in all the standard commentaries and histories of Israel. The following representative list is restricted to works which either are particularly significant or which include useful surveys of all the major arguments. The traditional date (458 BC) is favoured by:

Cross, 'A Reconstruction of the Judean Restoration'
In der Smitten, *Esra*, 91-105
U. Kellermann, 'Erwägungen zum Problem der Esradatierung', *ZAW* 80 (1968), 55-87 (Kellermann argues for a slightly later date, but still before Nehemiah)
Koch, 'Ezra and the Origins of Judaism'
J.S. Wright, *The Date of Ezra's Coming to Jerusalem*, 2nd edn, London: Tyndale Press, 1958

A date of 428 BC or thereabouts:

J. Bright, *A History of Israel*, 3rd edn, London: SCM, 1981, 391-402. This is the best and most readily available treatment of this view, though note also:
V. Pavlovský, 'Die Chronologie der Tätigkeit Esdras. Versuch einer neuen Lösung', *Biblica* 38 (1957), 275-305 and 428-56

This view was thoroughly examined by Emerton, to see in particular whether it is to be preferred to the later date:

J.A. Emerton, 'Did Ezra go to Jerusalem in 428 BC?', *JTS* n.s. 17 (1966), 1-19

The late date (398 BC) was first suggested by M. Vernes in 1889 and then more fully by A. Van Hoonacker in a long series of publications between 1890 and 1924. See more recently:

H. Cazelles, 'La Mission d'Esdras', *VT* 4 (1954), 113-40
Galling, *Studien*, 149-84
H.H. Rowley, 'The Chronological Order of Ezra and Nehemiah', in *The Servant of the Lord and Other Essays*, 2nd edn, Oxford: Blackwell, 1965, 137-68
Widengren, 'The Persian Period', 503-509

One of the particular arguments which advocates of the late date frequently advance is examined critically by:

> J.R. Porter, 'Son or Grandson (Ezra x.6)?', *JTS* n.s. 17 (1966), 54-67

Other articles referred to in the course of this discussion:

> B. Porten, 'Aramaic Papyri and Parchments: a New Look', *BA* 49 (1979), 74-104
>
> H.G.M. Williamson, 'The Historical Value of Josephus' *Jewish Antiquities* xi. 297-301', *JTS* n.s. 28 (1977), 49-66

D. Ezra's Mission

Historians of the Biblical period are frequently confronted with the problem that their major source—the Bible itself—was not generally written with their type of questions in mind. Whereas Nehemiah's account is relatively straightforward, and so does not need further discussion here, Ezra's mission to Jerusalem typifies this dilemma; as a result, it has evoked a number of speculations concerning his status, his personal motivation, his achievements and his demise.

In looking briefly at each of these, it will again be helpful to bear in mind the results of our literary analysis—in this case, in particular, the conclusion that a first-person account by Ezra has been rearranged and edited in various places. As a rough and ready guide, we may say that editorial activity (and hence ideology) is likely to be most apparent in the passages which have been rewritten in the third person, namely, Ezra 7.1-11; 8.35-36; 10; and Neh. 8 (the basis of which came between Ezra 8 and 9 in the first-person account). (We have also suggested that material which once came at Ezra 10.16 underlies Neh. 9.1-5, but that is hardly of importance for us here.) Of course, those whose understanding of the nature and growth of the literature is different will necessarily offer an alternative historical narrative. Broadly speaking, the historical outline of an ultra-conservative will scarcely depart from a retelling of the Biblical story. A radical critic will be sceptical about any historical reconstruction and will explain most of the material as later interpretation (but of what?). The approach favoured here, needless to say, seeks to steer a middle course: there is a good deal that we can learn about the historical Ezra, but interpretation of his role and significance has inevitably been programmed into the text by the work of the later editor(s). This was a process which then continued for centuries

after, as we know from the number of apocryphal and pseudepi-
graphical works named after him. And so to the four points listed
above.

(a) Discussion of Ezra's status focuses on an influential monograph
by H.H. Schaeder. Schaeder was one of those few scholars who are at
home both in Iranian and Old Testament studies. Consequently,
there are aspects of his theory which most of the rest of us have to
accept on trust. He argued that the description of Ezra as 'the scribe
of the law of the God of heaven' in Artaxerxes' edict (Ezra 7.12) was
an official Persian title. On this view, Ezra was an important civil
servant at the Achaemenid court with responsibility for the handling
of all matters relating to the Jewish community in their relationship
with the imperial crown. It is thus quite common to find him referred
to in textbooks as the minister or secretary of state for Jewish affairs.
In consequence, Ezra may himself have proposed to the king that his
mission to Jerusalem would be desirable, and he may even have been
responsible for drafting his own authorization in the king's name in
the edict of Ezra 7.12-26.

It is not necessary to be an expert in Iranian to realize that this
attractive proposal cannot but be hypothetical for at least two
reasons. First, we are told nothing directly about Ezra's status at the
Achaemenid court. The title itself is not Iranian in wording, unlike
the difficult Iranian loan-words at Ezra 4.8-9 and 5.6. Second, the
possibility must be remembered that the edict could as well be
investing Ezra with his authority as building upon it. Thus although
it is very probable that Ezra was a prominent leader of the Jewish
community in Babylon, a sober historian must be prepared to say
that his sources do not permit him to say anything more for certain
about Ezra's official status there.

What does seem clear, however, is that when the later editor
described him as 'a scribe who was skilled in the law of Moses which
the Lord, the God of Israel, had given' (7.6, and cf. 7.10 and 11), he
was certainly interpreting Ezra's role in the light of Ezra's subsequent
ministry. Civil authority has here disappeared completely from view,
and Ezra is already assuming the mantle of a great religious leader,
someone more akin to the later rabbis as an expositor of the word of
God for the community of the faithful.

(b) We move on to consider next what evidence there is to establish how Ezra himself may have regarded his mission. This is necessary because in an attractive article Koch has advanced three bold hypotheses which we may summarize in his own words. (i) 'Ezra's march from Babylonia to Jerusalem was a cultic procession which Ezra understood as a second Exodus and a partial fulfilment of prophetic expectations.' (ii) 'Ezra came to Jerusalem as the real high priest of the family of Aaron. His purpose was to change his people into a "holy seed" around the holy place, which God had given as a tent-peg and source of life during the times of political servitude.' (iii) 'Ezra was sent "to all his 'people beyond the river'"', including the Samaritans. His aim was to establish one Israel out of all 12 tribes, which explains the later acceptance of the Pentateuch by the Samaritans.'

This is heady stuff! And Koch argues his case with great erudition and a lively attention to detail. Nevertheless, the need for caution should at once be realized when we observe that many of the most important supporting arguments which Koch adduces are in fact based on the third-person passages in the Ezra material. For instance, Ezra's genealogy with its high-priestly overtones in Ezra 7.1-5 is poorly integrated into its context, as the resumptive 'this Ezra' at the start of v. 6 shows. It is probable, as most commentators agree, that it owes its presence here to the later editor, and not to Ezra himself. Again, as we have already seen, the eulogistic description of Ezra in 7.6 and 10 is more likely the editor's reflection on Ezra's role than his personal self-appraisal. Other parts of Koch's theory, such as Ezra's relations with those who resided beyond the borders of Judah, may be interpreted with greater historical probability in other ways, as we shall see shortly. Finally, Koch's theory is unlikely as an explanation for the Samaritans' acceptance of the Pentateuch, for in their own literature they vilify few others as vehemently as Ezra. If, as I believe, the religious community of the Samaritans was not established until later and included amongst its early founders a dissident group of liberal-minded priests from Jerusalem, their acceptance of the Pentateuch should cause no surprise.

Without going through all Koch's arguments in detail, we may nevertheless conclude that he has confused later pious and idealizing interpretation with historical actuality. That Ezra regarded his company as in some sense representing 'Israel' is not unlikely. That he came with high expectations which in the event could not be fully realized is only to be expected. But that he failed so catastrophically as Koch's hypothesis seems to entail makes difficult the very reputation which he later acquired and which Koch seems anxious to safeguard.

(c) Third, then, why was Ezra sent to Jerusalem, and to what extent was he successful in his objectives? To probe these questions, our starting point, as most scholars agree, must be the plain statements of Artaxerxes' edict rather than speculations about some unexpressed hidden agenda. According to the text of the edict, Ezra was sent with four objectives which we may conveniently examine in turn.

(i) Ezra was sent first in order to lead back to Judah any of the Jews in Babylon who wished to return (7.13). As we have seen, this was a politically understandable move on Artaxerxes' part, and it is generally thought probable that there were more such returns during the first century or so of Achaemenid rule than our present texts refer to.

In spelling out how he successfully accomplished this task (Ezra 8), Ezra expresses particular concern that there should be at least a token group of Levites in the party. Here we may accept Koch's suggestion that 'Exodus typology' is involved. Since the Levites were responsible for all the cultic paraphernalia during the journey through the wilderness after the first Exodus, Ezra will have considered their involvement appropriate here as well in view of the treasures which had been entrusted to him for the service of the temple. We have already noted, however (and will see again in Chapter 4), that this understanding was also characteristic of the earlier return (Ezra 1), so that it should not be singled out as something unique to Ezra.

(ii) Ezra was charged next with the safe transportation of various gifts and grants from the king and others for the temple (Ezra 7.15ff.). This, too, has well-attested precedents (Ezra 1.7-11 and 6.1-10 etc.), and Achaemenid support of other local cults is not unknown.

This part of his commission was also scrupulously carried out by Ezra. His detailed description of his accounting procedures (8.24-30 and 33-34) has all the hallmarks of one who knows how quickly suspicions of corruption can be aroused in the minds of those who have entrusted large sums of money to another party.

(iii) Ezra's next task is not quite so easy to understand. 'You are sent by the king and his seven counsellors to conduct an inquiry into the situation in Judah and Jerusalem on the basis of the law of your God which is in your hand' (7.14). What was the scope and purpose of this inquiry? Neither the edict nor the subsequent narrative gives us a firm answer, but there are some hints.

First, the continuation of the edict deals in considerable detail with concern for the worship in the Jerusalem temple. In view of Achaemenid interest in the religious well-being of their subject peoples, attested, for instance, in the Passover Papyrus (*AP* 21), Ezra's inquiry may have been aimed primarily at investigating (and, by implication, improving where necessary) the conformity of the temple cult with the Mosaic law as its officially recognized constitution. In particular, before the recurrent grants and concessions of 7.17 and 21-24 could be renewed, the king would have wished to be satisfied that the expenditure was being properly administered. No doubt he considered that this was a potentially sound investment both politically and for personal religious reasons (cf. 6.10 and the Cyrus Cylinder, *ANET*, p. 316, for earlier, and *AP* 30.25-26 for later parallels). 7.23 drops a broad hint in this direction.

Second, it is possible that the amount of space devoted in Ezra's account to the problem of mixed marriages may find its explanation at one level in this same concern. The size and membership of the community centred round the temple would obviously need to be carefully determined, and cases of mixed marriages would pose a particular difficulty in this regard. It may not be coincidental, therefore, that the whole affair came to a head in 10.16 with a group of prominent citizens who sat with Ezra 'to examine the matter'. Ezra's personal concerns may well have gone beyond the more circumscribed considerations of the king, but here too he may have been attempting to conform his activities as far as possible to the terms of the edict.

(iv) The last item with which Artaxerxes charged Ezra is the most controversial of all. According to Ezra 7.25-26, he was to 'appoint magistrates and judges to judge all the people in Beyond the River, that is to say all those who practise the laws of your God; and you must instruct any who do not acknowledge them'. Ezra is then given authority to punish any who do not obey this requirement, summarized as 'the law of your God and the law of the king'. Assuming that this is an authentic part of the edict, how should we understand it?

Probably the majority of commentators treat these verses as an amplification of v. 14, just discussed. They think that in reality it still refers to the Judaean community, since nowhere else would its terms have been applicable. Against this, however, it must be observed that 'to conduct an inquiry' (v. 14) is a far more limited exercise than that envisaged here; that it would be surprising if in an official document no difference were intended between 'Judah and Jerusalem' (v. 14) and 'Beyond the River' (v. 25); that there is no good reason why this passage is separated so far from the verse it is intended to explain; and that historically speaking it is improbable that there were no groups outside Judah who did not regard themselves as living under 'the law of the God of Heaven'.

Should we then go as far as the minority of scholars who, like Ackroyd (and to some extent Koch), think that the text envisages 'a situation in which the whole province becomes one community, all obedient to the law'? This view is also hard to accept in historical terms. The province of Beyond the River was far more extensive than the former kingdoms of Israel and Judah, and its inhabitants were of very varied backgrounds. It can hardly be supposed that anyone ever thought that they would all submit themselves to the Jewish law whilst still being part of the Persian empire. Besides, since 'all the people' is explained as 'all those who practise the laws of your God', it is likely that 'any who do not acknowledge them' should be understood to mean 'any who do not acknowledge this law, but who ought to on account of their background'.

A third possibility should thus be explored. If Ezra's inquiry (v. 14) has been correctly understood, it clearly relates primarily to the inhabitants of Judah, for whom the temple was the focal point of community life. As had already been envisaged in Deuteronomy, however, the religious life of those who lived at some distance from the central sanctuary had perforce to be organized along somewhat different lines. It would not in any way be contrary to Achaemenid policy to suggest that Ezra was to instruct such groups in how they should apply the law to themselves in their different circumstances. Of course, since the Mosaic law legislates for both civil and religious conduct without distinction, this could be a delicate matter. Who better, then, to establish such guidelines than a leading representative of Babylonian Jewry, where a *modus vivendi* of this sort must have long since been established? There can have been few who understood better than Ezra how to reconcile the sometimes conflicting demands of 'the law of your God and the law of the king' (v. 26).

Ezra's account gives no hint that he made any progress towards implementing this programme. It is true that he made important strides in teaching the law (Neh. 8) and in introducing methods of interpretation which we shall examine in Chapter 4. But so far as we know, this was confined to Judah alone, and of the institutions intended to safeguard his programme for the future (the magistrates and judges) we hear nothing. So what happened? This brings us neatly to the final point listed above for historical consideration.

(d) We have already noted more than once that Ezra's recorded ministry spans just twelve months. If that was the total duration of his commission, or if he was required to account for his stewardship after that period, it is scarcely surprising that he did not succeed in achieving all that he set out to do. By the same token, however, we might have expected Artaxerxes to give him longer to do his work.

Now, on the chronology for which we have argued above, it is clear from the end of Ezra 4 that at about this time things began to go badly wrong in Judah. (Note that the reference in 4.12 to 'the Jews who came up from you to us' can be most naturally understood as Ezra's caravan.) An attempt to rebuild the walls of Jerusalem aroused the suspicions of various other local officials in the Satrapy. They persuaded the king that this was a seditious move, and in view of the troubled times through which that whole area of the empire had recently been passing he ordered the work to be immediately stopped 'lest the threat grow to the point of damaging the royal interests' (4.22).

Although there have been occasional suggestions that Ezra was directly involved in this wall-building, it is important to be clear in our minds that there is no evidence for this whatsoever, and the theory is improbable. Nor do we for one moment believe that the Jews were really planning the rebellion of which they were accused. What we may reasonably conclude, however, is that Artaxerxes' attitude towards Judah must have been strongly influenced in a negative manner by the report he had received and that this is likely to have remained the situation until Nehemiah was able to use his personal position to effect a change. In these circumstances, any activity of Ezra beyond the province of Judah would have been out of the question. If he was still working in Jerusalem at the time (which

we do not know), it is probable that he would have been called to
account and his authority severely curtailed, if not withdrawn. Thus
even if his ministry lasted more than a year, we can see that external
pressures must have prevented him from seeing his commission
through to completion. The very most we could say is that if Ezra
took part in the later ceremony to dedicate the wall which Nehemiah
built (cf. Neh. 12.36—but most commentators regard his name there
as a later editorial insertion), then he may have continued to live in
Jerusalem as a senior and respected 'elder statesman'.

Are we then justified in saying that Ezra failed? Viewed in one
light, we must conclude that he did not accomplish everything that
he was sent to do, and that for good reasons. The present text
suggests, however, that Ezra did not consider this his most important
task. As the later editor comments, 'Ezra had committed himself to
the study of the law of the Lord and its practice and to the teaching of
statute and ordinance in Israel' (7.10). Judged by this criterion, Ezra
was brilliantly successful. As the editor has underlined by giving
Nehemiah 8 its new climactic position, Ezra established the law as
the basis for the life of all the people. He rescued it from the danger
of falling into neglect on account of changed political circumstances,
and paved the way for its acceptance as in some sense a timeless
document. The later reforms in Nehemiah's day, the work of our
editor after that, and the very history of Judaism itself demonstrate
that he gave a direction to the life of his people which was to outlast
by far the imperial power which had initially commissioned him.

Further Reading

H.L. Ellison, 'The Importance of Ezra', *EvQ* 53 (1981), 48-53
Galling, *Studien*, 149-84
A.H.J. Gunneweg, 'Zur Interpretation der Bücher Esra–Nehemia',
     SVT 32 (1981), 146-61
In der Smitten, *Esra*
Koch, 'Ezra and the Origins of Judaism'
Mowinckel, *Studien III*
Schaeder, *Esra der Schreiber*
Wright, *The Date of Ezra's Coming to Jerusalem*

4

THEOLOGY

FOR MANY years now there has been a long-running debate about how best to organize and arrange a 'Theology of the Old Testament'—always assuming, of course, that it is legitimate to draw together into a synthesis the many different voices which come to us from such varied backgrounds over a period of a thousand years or more. Traditionally, the major headings of Christian systematic theology have been used: God, creation, man, sin, salvation, life as the people of God, and eschatology. It is self-evident, however, that the Old Testament itself is not arranged according to these categories. As a result, proposals are regularly put forward which aim to do greater justice to the way in which the Old Testament presents itself to its readers.

Amongst the many difficulties which the Old Testament raises in this area is its widespread use of narrative, for it is not always easy to know how to use narrative texts for theological reflection. An additional problem in the case of Ezra and Nehemiah is their comparatively late date relative to the Old Testament as a whole. How much of what precedes do they take for granted? Are they merely reasserting long-held values and beliefs, or are they developing them? Alternatively, are they attempting to correct and redirect the age-old faith of the people of Israel for the new conditions which prevailed in the post-exilic period? The danger of bringing traditional categories to bear on these books is that we may thereby overlook the possibly distinctive emphases of their presentation. On the other hand, to concentrate exclusively on the points at which they differ from the other writings in the Old Testament may distort our understanding by ignoring the importance which they attach to fundamental issues which they take for granted.

A final area of uncertainty is raised by the diverse nature of the sources which we have unearthed. We cannot assume, for instance, that the historical figures of Ezra and Nehemiah necessarily shared identical beliefs and outlooks, or that the editor who combined their accounts inevitably agreed wholeheartedly with either or both of them. So whose 'theology' are we trying to describe?

In seeking to come to terms in a responsible manner with these disconcerting observations, a few guidelines may be suggested. First, it would seem to be most sensible to begin with what we now have—the finished product of what is, in reality, a single book. It would not have been impossible for its editor(s) to have made a different selection of source material, or to have arranged this material in a different order. The study of the present arrangement of a Biblical book is known as redaction criticism, and it seems to many that it is the most reliable guide to the central concerns of a given work.

Second, however, it needs to be emphasized that the kind of literary and historical inquiry which has dominated our thinking in the preceding chapters of this book cannot suddenly be swept under the carpet when we start to think theologically. Rather, it is only as we keep them firmly in the forefront of our minds that the particular interests of the editors who gave the final shape to this book stand out most clearly.

Finally, in order to maintain a right balance between conservatism and innovation on the part of our authors, we shall need to be sensitive in particular to the way in which they handle familiar themes. Just because an older law is cited, for instance, it does not immediately follow that the law is being understood and applied in precisely the same way as it was in the pre-exilic period. Careful exegesis of each example within what we know of the prevailing historical and ideological context must determine our appreciation of the writers' theology.

In this chapter, an attempt will be made to outline what, in the light of these guidelines, appear to me to be the major theological concerns of Ezra and Nehemiah. In order to keep the discussion clear, I shall assume the literary and historical conclusions already arrived at. It is no use pretending, however, that a different set of conclusions would not entail the modification of this presentation at a number of points.

A. The Development of a History of Salvation

The books of Ezra and Nehemiah describe the physical and spiritual restoration and reorganization of the Judaean community after the Babylonian exile. Historically, this took place over more than a century, though the sources which were available for the description of this lengthy period span only a handful of years. There is reference to the first year of Cyrus's reign (Ezra 1.1), the rebuilding of the temple in the reign of Darius (although this lasted some five years, the whole account centres around the report of Tattenai's inquiry in Ezra 5-6), the mission of Ezra, which lasted one year early in Artaxerxes I's reign, an exchange of letters with doleful consequences (Ezra 4.7-23), the first year of Nehemiah's governorship, during which he rebuilt the wall, and some isolated events from his second term as governor, perhaps fifteen years later. The remaining tatters of information are of indeterminate date and in any case they do not amount to very much.

Judged from an historical point of view, it is impossible for the most part to detect any continuity between these isolated incidents in terms of cause and effect. The Jewish community obviously did not have a blueprint for restoration towards which the reformers were working as and when they were able.

As presented in the books of Ezra and Nehemiah, however, the pattern of restoration is far from haphazard and no phase of it is left any more in isolation. On the contrary, the rigid constraints of chronology with which we are familiar here recede into the background whilst continuity and purpose at the level of divine causality receive a heavy emphasis. Noteworthy instances of this radical bridging operation include the following: (i) the rebuilding of the temple is summarized in Ezra 6.14 with these words: 'The elders of the Jews went on successfully with the building under the prophesying of Haggai the prophet and Zechariah the son of Iddo, and they completed the building according to the command of the God of Israel and the decree of Cyrus and Darius and Artaxerxes the king of Persia'. We have argued that the author of these words was one of the last to contribute to the book as a whole and that he already had in front of him the account of Ezra's and Nehemiah's ministry. His reference to all three Persian kings who play a major part in the history shows that he is standing back somewhat from the ebb and flow of the historical continuum and regarding the whole task of temple restoration as a single event in response to 'the command of the God of Israel'. The earliest return under Cyrus, the major rebuilding under Darius and the further provision which Artaxerxes made through Ezra (cf. 7.15ff. and especially 7.27) are here grouped together as one. The particularly remarkable point, of course, and one which has caused difficulties for the commentators, is the reference to Artaxerxes when the narrative has only reached as far as the reign of Darius. Indeed, the NEB goes so far as to omit the reference to Artaxerxes altogether. But this problem recedes in the light of our present approach. The editor of Ezra 1–6 has already shown in Ezra 4 that he can group by theme rather than strict chronology, for there his account of the opposition was traced down as far as Artaxerxes. It is thus entirely fitting that his appreciation of the divine benevolence in restoration should do the same.

(ii) The account of Ezra's activity is introduced in 7.1 with the initially startling words, 'Now after these things'. Who would guess that this seemingly casual remark spans a gap of more than fifty years? In the divine economy, however, Ezra's ministry was the next significant step. Theologically, therefore, the remark is wholly appropriate. The same outlook may also be reflected in Ezra's genealogy which immediately follows, for Seraiah, whose son Ezra is said to be, was apparently the high priest just before the exile to Babylon (cf. 1 Chron. 6.14).

(iii) The interweaving of the accounts of Ezra and Nehemiah by the inclusion of Ezra material at Neh. 8 further serves to bind together the historically separate steps in the restoration. We have already noted how materials of quite diverse origin have been combined in Neh. 8–10 to forge an account of covenant renewal as a major climax to the work of these two leading figures.

(iv) The lists of priests and Levites in Neh. 12.1-26 also serve as an organic link between the various phases covered by the books as a whole, and this is emphasized by the concluding summary in v. 26. 'These served in the days of Joiakim, son of Jeshua' puts us in touch with the generation of the first return, while 'and in the days of Nehemiah the governor and of Ezra the priest (and) scribe' brings us down without a gap to the later work of the two reformers.

(v) Finally, Neh. 12.47, with its reference to 'all Israel in the days of Zerubbabel, and in the days of Nehemiah', serves exactly the same function.

The passages singled out for particular comment here may be taken as highlighting what was undoubtedly the view of the book's editors overall. Historically time-bound events are becoming detached from their chronological moorings in order to be viewed rather as divinely related steps in what may properly be regarded as a history of salvation. This is a term which is more commonly used of the much earlier phases in the formation of Israel herself—of the Exodus and conquest narratives, for instance. Here too, many scholars believe that these records unite traditions which were originally quite separate, whilst others, particularly when they first encounter such views, are resistant to the suggestion because of their apparently radical historical consequences. In Ezra and Nehemiah, however, the issues are relatively clear-cut, and the processes by which the literature developed lie closer to the surface. It may be suggested, therefore, that in this area too they afford a more readily intelligible way in to the methods of Old Testament theological narrative.

Further Reading

Childs, *Introduction*, 624-38
Gunneweg, 'Zur Interpretation der Bücher Esra-Nehemia'

B. Continuity and Legitimation

Having taken note of the general manner in which the books of Ezra and Nehemiah present the period of return and restoration, it is necessary to ask next how this whole episode was considered to have fitted into God's dealings with Israel. In order to appreciate their contribution to this issue, we need to face squarely the radical discontinuity between the pre- and post-exilic periods.

When Jerusalem fell to the Babylonian king Nebuchadnezzar, scarcely any of the national institutions of Judah survived unscathed. (The northern kingdom of Israel had, of course, long since passed from the pages of history as an independent entity.) National sovereignty disappeared as Judah was absorbed into the Babylonian empire. In tandem with this, the Davidic king Zedekiah was led ignominiously in chains to Babylon, where his predecessor Jehoiachin was already in prison. The land of God's promise no longer provided a setting in which his people could freely serve him, for many of them, especially their leaders, were likewise physically removed to Babylon, whilst the land itself, as already mentioned, passed into foreign hands. Jerusalem, or, more poignantly, Mount Zion, the city of the Great King (Ps. 48.2), lay in ruins whilst the temple, focal point of the nation's worship, was first robbed of all its treasures and then destroyed. In human terms, nothing remained of a once independent nation. Something of the despair of the times may be gauged from the book of Lamentations, whilst contemporary prophets such as Ezekiel made clear that there could be no straight path back to the situation which had formerly prevailed.

As we know with historical hindsight, however, Israel as a religious community refused to die. But by what right could that later religious community centred around a new temple in Jerusalem lay claim to stand in direct descent from the earlier nation? How should they resolve their identity crisis now that the prevailing political circumstances had been so radically, and, it appeared, so irrevocably, changed? The books of Ezra and Nehemiah set out to answer some of these questions by emphasizing certain lines of continuity with the earlier history whilst at the same time soft-pedalling various others, regarding them as blind alleys.

Continuity is underlined in three main ways. One of these concerns the status and application of the written law of God, and to this we shall devote a separate section later. The other two are the tracing of links between the institutions of the post-exilic community and their pre-exilic counterparts, and the use of typology as a method for interpreting the significance of historical events.

1. *Lines of institutional continuity*

The most obvious institutional link with the earlier period was the temple in Jerusalem and the forms of worship centred upon it. Time and again these books emphasize that this was no 'new temple but simply the Solomonic temple rebuilt on its site' (Clines, p. 25). The altar was first restored 'on its original site' (Ezra 3.3), and the same concern was emphasized with regard to the building as a whole. In the record of Cyrus's original decree in Ezra 6, it is probable that we should translate 6.3*b*, 'Let the house be rebuilt on the place where they used to offer sacrifices and let its foundations be retained'. When Darius reaffirmed Cyrus's intention, he too underlined the same point by confirming the right of the Jews to 'rebuild this house of God on its original site' (6.7). Similar wording is also used in this connection at 2.68 and 5.11 and 15.

The plans for the construction of the second temple also mirrored those of the first. It is generally agreed that the obviously damaged text of Ezra 6.3c should be restored to read, 'Its height shall be thirty cubits, its length sixty cubits and its width twenty cubits', and this exactly corresponds to the dimensions of the first temple as recorded in 1 Kgs 6.2. The method of construction too is the same: 'three courses of dressed stone and one course of timber' (Ezra 6.4, and cf. 5.8) is identical to the first temple; cf. 1 Kgs 6.36 and 7.12.

The writers apparently ascribed particular importance to the fact that the vessels used in the service of the second temple were the very ones which Nebuchadnezzar had carried off to Babylon and which Cyrus had had carefully taken back: note the studied wording to this effect at Ezra 1.7-8; 5.14-15; 6.5. (The vessels mentioned in Ezra 7.19 and 8.25-27, by contrast, appear to have been newly made as part of Artaxerxes' grant to Ezra.) The importance of these vessels was twofold. On the one hand, they provided a tangible point of contact with the temple worship of the pre-exilic period. On the other hand, they had a symbolic value in the context of exile and restoration: normally, victorious kings in the ancient Near East removed the images of the gods of those whom they had defeated and placed them in their own temples to underline the superiority of the god of the conquerors. This option was not available in the case of the Jews, however, and so Nebuchadnezzar put these vessels 'in the temple of his god' (Ezra 1.7) in Babylon instead. Their return by Cyrus was thus of particular significance in the context of restoration.

Not only the building and its furnishing, but also the personnel who served in the temple are said to be in a direct line of continuity with earlier times. The references back to Moses and David in Ezra 6.18 and Neh. 12.24 and 45-46 are especially instructive here, but a similar concern may also account for parts of the lists and genealogies which the editors have included in these books.

Finally, the cultic practices themselves conform either explicitly or by implication to those of earlier times: see, for instance, Ezra 3.3-6, 10-11; 6.19-20; 8.35; Neh. 8.13-18; 10.29-39; 13.10-14; etc. In particular, the description of the dedication ceremony for the second temple is probably intended to evoke that for the first in Solomon's day (1 Kgs 8).

Another major source of continuity is provided by the genealogical purity of the people themselves. This is an aspect of Ezra and Nehemiah which many modern readers find unattractive, for it seems to smack of racial pride and superiority. Without doubt it needs to be balanced by many other parts of the Old Testament which resolutely adopt a more open stance towards both the Gentile nations and the other groups of descendants from pre-exilic Israel which had not shared in the Babylonian exile. For the moment, however, it will suffice for our purposes to acknowledge that there is also a positive side to such lists as those in Ezra 2 and Neh. 7, namely the claim that physically speaking the new community is but the old reconstituted. Where this could not be immediately established for certain, the policy was to keep the families concerned in a state of limbo until further evidence was forthcoming (cf. Ezra 2.59-63). It is reassuring to learn that in at least one case, that of the family of Hakkoz, this had been resolved in a positive fashion by the time Ezra came to Jerusalem (cf. Ezra 8.33 with Neh. 3.4 and 21). What is more, it was also possible for those who had never been in exile to be reintegrated into the temple community, which regarded itself as in some measure representative of all Israel (cf. Ezra 6.21). Indeed, we have already noted (Chapter 1 §D (2)) Japhet's recent suggestion that the association in Ezra 2 of those identified by family association and those identified by place of domicile testifies to a desire to amalgamate into one the two communities of the exiles and those who had remained in the land.

Finally, although the land does not receive overt attention in these books as a token of continuity, it is no doubt to be so regarded. The emphasis on the importance of 'return', and the fact that the community regularly style themselves as 'the exiles' or the like (e.g. Ezra 1.11; 2.1; 3.8; 6.19 and 21; Neh. 1.3, etc.), testify to the underlying assumption that the restoration took place in the setting of the land which God promised to Israel. Indeed, this conviction comes to prominent expression in the prayers of Ezra 9 and Neh. 9, and in the latter it is the springboard for forward-looking hopes that God may yet work to restore the freedom in the land which was once enjoyed and whose lack is still so keenly felt.

2. *Typology*

By 'typology' in this context we mean the use of language in the description of one event which consciously evokes another earlier event of significance in the history of the people. Not surprisingly, the most prominent example of this in Ezra and Nehemiah is the patterning of the return from Babylon on the accounts of the Exodus from Egypt and related events, and we shall therefore concentrate on that alone here.

There are three examples of this device in the very first chapter of Ezra. First, the statement in v. 11 that the exiles 'were brought up from Babylon to Jerusalem' reminds us of an earlier and frequently repeated formula, as when God speaks to Moses of 'the people whom you have brought up from the land of Egypt unto the land which I promised to Abraham. . .' (Exod. 33.1; cf. Gen. 50.24; Exod. 3.8, 17; etc.). Second, the wording of v. 6 suggests that the writer has in mind the theme of the 'despoiling of the Egyptians', which features prominently in the account of the Exodus (cf. Exod. 3.21-22; 11.2; 12.35-36; Ps. 105.37). Third, the theme of the return of the temple vessels in vv. 7-11, already discussed, was probably also intended by the author to contribute to this picture. Whilst the transportation of sacred vessels was not an overt part of the Exodus account itself, it is clear from Isa. 52.11-12 that it had become part of the prophetic complex of motifs looking forward to the return from Babylon as a second exodus. If so, then the further suggestion may be advanced that Sheshbazzar's enigmatic title, 'the prince of Judah' (Ezra 1.8), may not have anything to do with his political status, but rather be a recollection of the lists of 'princes' of the various tribes of Israel in the book of Numbers (2.3-31; 7.1-83; 34.18-28), and in particular of Num. 7.84-86 where these 'princes' are associated with a number of gold and silver vessels given for the dedication of the altar.

In such ways as these, then, our author presents the return from Babylon as a 'second exodus', an act of God's grace comparable with the very birth of the nation itself. From an historical point of view it is likely that the return was a long drawn out and rather unspectacular affair. The use of typology, however, opens the eye of faith to the hand of God behind the historical process. To those who may have been tempted to play down the significance of what had happened, our author invites the thought that it may be described as no less than a rebirth of the nation.

The case is not dissimilar in the description of Ezra's later return in Ezra 7-8. We have already noted, when dealing with Koch's analysis, that some of the points, especially in ch.8, probably derive from Ezra's own understanding of his journey, and that these have been reinforced by his later editor. The language of 'going up' in Ezra 7.6-9 is suggestive, and he seems to find particular significance in the date on which Ezra planned to begin his journey—'the first day of the first month' (Ezra 7.9). If, as v. 10 suggests, Ezra chose this date because of his study of the Torah, it was doubtless because of reflection in particular upon the date in Exod. 12.2.

As presented in this book, therefore, the second exodus is not a solitary event, but the type of experience which successive generations may enjoy. Its promise and hope were not exhausted by the first group who returned. Rather, the prospect of a renewed life confronted each successive generation with its challenge for decision, not unlike the repeated Deuteronomic exhortation to all second generations to 'choose life' (Deut. 30.15-20; and cf. 5.3 etc.).

We may thus conclude that by emphasizing continuity with the past and by establishing a framework within which to interpret their own recent history, the authors of Ezra and Nehemiah endeavoured to encourage their contemporaries to regard themselves as the direct heirs of pre-exilic Israel.

Further Reading

P.R. Ackroyd, 'God and People in the Chronicler's Presentation of Ezra', in J. Coppens (ed.), *La notion biblique de Dieu*, Leuven: University Press, 1976, 145-62

P.R. Ackroyd, 'The Temple Vessels—A Continuity Theme', *SVT* 23 (1972), 166-81

Japhet, 'People and Land in the Restoration Period'

Koch, 'Ezra and the Origins of Judaism'

G. von Rad, *Das Geschichtsbild des chronistischen Werkes* (BWANT 54), Stuttgart: Kohlhammer, 1930

H.C.M. Vogt, *Studie zur nachexilischen Gemeinde in Esra-Nehemia*, Werl: Dietrich Coelde, 1966

C. **God, King and Nation**

Our examination of the theology of Ezra and Nehemiah so far has suggested that these books aim to present the various phases of the restoration as parts of a single act of God, who had moved to reestablish the post-exilic community as the legitimate heir and successor of pre-exilic Israel. In response, and as a climax to the work of renewal and reform, the people had entered into a solemn pledge 'to live by God's law which was given through Moses . . . and carefully to obey all the commandments, judgements and statutes of the Lord' (Neh. 10.29) with particular attention to the maintenance of the temple with its cultus and personnel. This was intended, we need not doubt, to give to the first readers a firm self-awareness and sense of identity within the age-old and continuing history of the relationship between God and his chosen people.

Alongside this diachronic dimension, however, there was also the need for an understanding of the synchronic aspects of their position: in particular, how should they regard their relationships with the dominant but foreign political rulers—the Persian, and later Hellenistic, imperial authorities at the court, and the local officials with whom they came into more immediate and regular contact? An important corollary of this question was their position vis-à-vis the pre-exilic institutions of government and in particular the Davidic monarchy, about which God had made such far-reaching promises. Ought they now to look for, and perhaps even actively work for, a restoration of the monarchy, viewed as a further token of continuity, or had the political situation so changed that these promises were no longer applicable?

There is evidence that not all in the post-exilic community were in agreement about these pressing questions; indeed, despite important differences between them, the influential books of Plöger and Hanson both suggest that opinions polarized to the point where one may speak of two distinct 'parties'. One may be labelled theocratic, which in this context refers to those who believed that the Jews should accept the political status quo and concentrate on the development of an exclusively religious community. The opposing view can be called visionary or eschatological, and it represents the opinion of those who looked for the overthrow of foreign domination and the reestablishment of political independence under a Davidic king.

With the exception of only one or two passages, our books present a consistent approach to this cluster of issues. First, they affirm emphatically that God worked directly through the Persian kings for the benefit of his people, and thanksgiving is regularly offered to him in response. Taking up the prophetic hopes of Deutero-Isaiah in particular (cf. Isa. 41.2, 25; 44.28; 45.1 and especially 45.13; see also Jer. 51.1 and 11), Ezra 1.1 states that 'the Lord stirred up the spirit of Cyrus king of Persia' to issue his decree authorizing the return of the Jews to Jerusalem and the rebuilding of the temple. In Ezra 4.3 the builders willingly acknowledge this authorization by Cyrus. Darius's confirmation of the situation in Ezra 6 is also to be viewed in a positive light, for the sequel to his permission is followed by two clear statements to that effect—in 6.14, which we discussed earlier, and in

6.22. There can be little doubt, therefore, that the first section of the books has no hesitation in affirming that God used the Persian kings as his agents.

The same is true in the case of Ezra, where again in the text as we have it it is the Persian monarch who takes the initiative for Ezra's journey and who provides materially for it. In return, Ezra is pleased to acknowledge this fact both in his benediction at 8.27-28 and more extensively in his prayer at 9.6-15 (cf. especially v. 9).

Second, because the Persian kings are presented as the political agents through whom God is at work, there is a corresponding playing down of the secular status of the Jewish leaders themselves. Japhet has used this observation in an illuminating manner to explain why it is that, contrary to what we might expect from our knowledge of the contemporary prophet Haggai, Zerubbabel is nowhere explicitly called 'governor' in Ezra and Nehemiah. The same conclusion holds for Sheshbazzar, who is only styled 'governor' in one of the Aramaic sources at Ezra 5.14, but not once in the editor's own material (in Ezra 1, for instance). Similarly, we are told nothing of Ezra's secular status (though the punishments which he is authorized to administer in 7.26 imply that he wielded considerable authority), whilst Nehemiah too makes little of his rank as governor. He lets it slip in Neh. 5.15, as we saw earlier, but his dealings with his people throughout his memoir are based on moral rather than vested authority.

Against such a background, it is not surprising that the books of Ezra and Nehemiah show no interest in the fortunes of the Davidic house. Their stance is entirely one of political quietism. What matters is the temple as a focal point for the service of God and an obedient community in its support. If the political powers authorize and sustain its cultus, they may be accepted as fulfilling the role which our writers doubtless regarded as the most important function which the pre-exilic kings had to play. No change need be anticipated or encouraged.

The one discordant voice in this otherwise unanimous verdict comes in the prayer of Neh. 9. After a lengthy review of Israel's history, which concentrates in particular on the promise and gift of land, the prayer holds up to God the contradiction implied between his past dealings with his people and their present sorry plight as political 'slaves', who are obliged to pay much of the land's produce in tribute to a foreign overlord. In this chapter, Persian rule is viewed as oppressive and there is an urgency about the desire for change. In both respects, the chapter is untypical of the rest of the books, and it is almost certainly of independent origin (see Chapter 1 §C (1)). The fact that the editor included it as part of his climactic compilation in Neh. 8–10 should not be ignored, however. Just as the work as a whole tends to peter out with a sense that it will be hard to maintain the ideals of the past, as sketched in Neh. 12.44–13.3, so this chapter keeps alive an awareness that God's best is yet to be. In terms of the books as a whole, however, this voice is muted. In the days of benign Achaemenid rule there was no need for change; much later, the harsh repression of some of the Hellenistic rulers would heighten the emphasis given to this alternative theme.

Third, in contrast to the positive portrayal of the Persian kings, their local officials are generally viewed in a very poor light. A regular narrative pattern develops in these books whereby each step forward in the restoration is countered by foreign interference. This is clear at Ezra 4 and throughout Neh. 1–6 (cf. 2.10, 19; 4.1, 7; 6.1), while in Ezra's case it takes the somewhat different form of mixed marriages (Ezra 9.1ff.). Whatever may have been their motivation at the time, these officials are presented as stopping at nothing in their resistance to the work of God in Jerusalem. There is undoubtedly an apologetic note in the emphasis that all their attempts to accuse the Jews of sedition and rebellion are based on malicious lies (cf., for instance, Ezra 4.13 and 16; Neh. 6.6-7), supported on one occasion by bribery (Ezra 4.5). Indeed, Ezra 4 as a whole shows that it is only when the Jews are misrepresented by their enemies and do not have the opportunity to explain themselves that the Persian king authorizes action against them. Otherwise, as we have seen, the kings are fully favourable towards the Jews, and the Jews in turn are not slow to exploit their consequent legal rights as the ones who alone are entrusted with the work of restoration (see especially Ezra 4.3; 5.16-17; and Neh. 2.20). By showing that the difficulties which the post-exilic community encountered were due to corrupt local officialdom rather than to the Persian court as such, these books reinforce their case for loyalty to the imperial power itself.

Finally, however, it follows from this stance that a rigid separation is advocated between the Jewish community and its neighbours. Whether outsiders seek to gain entry by close identification with the community (e.g. Ezra 4.1-2), by marriage (as in Ezra 9.1-2 and Neh. 13.23-28) or by frontal assault, the Jewish response of resolute exclusion is consistently presented as the ideal. Positively, they maintain that they alone are the true and legitimate successors of Israel, and that their exclusive claims and rights have been upheld by the very highest Persian authorities; to admit others to their company would jeopardize their legal privileges. Negatively, they regard all foreigners as potentially threatening. The only way to maintain their true identity was to keep well apart from everyone, since otherwise they ran the danger of being quickly swamped by the larger numbers of those whose aims and ideals were incompatible with theirs. Unattractive as much of this may seem to us today, it is not hard to sympathize with the fears of an embattled and financially weak community as they sought to maintain against overwhelming odds the distinctiveness and purity of what they believed God had vouchsafed to them.

Further Reading

Coggins, *Haggai, Zechariah, Malachi*, ch. 6

P.D. Hanson, *The Dawn of Apocalyptic*, Philadelphia: Fortress, 1975

S. Japhet, 'Sheshbazzar and Zerubbabel—Against the Background of the Historical and Religious Tendencies of Ezra-Nehemiah', *ZAW* 94 (1982), 66-98

O. Plöger, *Theocracy and Eschatology*, Oxford: Blackwell, 1968

D. **The Book of the Law**

We turn finally to the subject which may be regarded as the single most influential theological topic treated in the books of Ezra and Nehemiah—the status and interpretation of the book of the law. At a number of places, this book is explicitly entitled 'the book of Moses' or equivalents (cf. Ezra 6.18; Neh. 8.1,14; 10.29; 13.1), and other references to the law book are probably to be understood in a similar fashion (e.g. at Ezra 7.10, 11 and 14). As such, it serves as a powerful mark of continuity with the Israel of earlier generations, whilst at the same time its provisions are regarded as determinative for the present life of the community. All the themes treated so far in this chapter thus come together at this point, whilst much that is characteristic of both later Judaism and Christianity flows directly from it.

1. *The Identification of the Book of the Law*

There is a preliminary critical issue which has provoked much discussion: what is the law book to which reference is so frequently made? This question should further be broken down into two, namely the identification of the law which the historical Ezra brought to Jerusalem, and that which is presupposed by our books as a whole. As the history of scholarship shows, a full answer to these questions would go far beyond the confines of the present work, because they take us into the enormous field of the composition of the Pentateuch as a whole. A brief summary of opinions must therefore suffice for the present.

As regards Ezra's law book, the traditional view both in antiquity (cf. 4 Ezra 14.19-48) and since has been that the book is to all intents and purposes identical with the Pentateuch as we know it. Since the rise of modern critical scholarship, many have continued to maintain this view, arguing that Ezra or someone close to him was responsible for the final major phase in the Pentateuch's composition, the incorporation of the Priestly source into the earlier narrative and legal materials. Others, however, believe that the final redaction of the Pentateuch cannot have taken place as early as this view implies. They prefer to think either that Ezra brought with him the Priestly source itself as a separate document, or that he worked on the basis of Deuteronomy alone.

A decision on this matter has to be based primarily on an identification of the passages which Ezra either cites or alludes to, and this in turn involves a prior decision about what can be known of the historical Ezra himself. For instance, because Kellermann believes that only the edict of Artaxerxes in Ezra 7.12-26 gives us reliable historical information, he is able to identify Ezra's law-book with Deuteronomy; apparent references elsewhere to the priestly material in the Pentateuch (generally referred to as 'P') are all to be attributed to the Chronicler's midrashic expansion of this source.

By contrast, we have argued above that far more should be ascribed to the Ezra source than Kellermann's minimalist conclusions allow. In particular, we shall seek to show below that Ezra 9.1-2 and Neh. 8.13-18 make use both of Deuteronomy and of P. The same is true of the various clauses in the pledge of Neh. 10, whilst all agree that the long historical survey in the prayer of Neh. 9 draws without distinction on all the major Pentateuchal sources as normally defined. As a working hypothesis, therefore, it seems preferable to maintain that both Ezra himself and the later editors of these books made use of the Pentateuch as a whole.

It cannot be proved on the basis of a few citations and allusions, of course, that the law book was identical with the present form of the Pentateuch in every detail. Many find significant, for instance, the lack of reference to the Day of Atonement (Lev. 16) in Neh. 8, for in the cultic calendar of Lev. 23 this comes on the tenth day of the month, between the Feast of Trumpets on the first day (cf. Neh. 8.1-12) and the Feast of Tabernacles, which started on the fifteenth day (cf. Neh. 8.13-18). It is possible, therefore, that it had not yet been included in the law which Ezra presented. Personally, I favour the alternative explanation that it is not mentioned in Neh. 8 because it was not relevant to the concerns of that chapter as a whole, but even without that our general conclusion will not be seriously affected. It requires only that we allow that certain modifications were made to the Pentateuch after Ezra's time.

In recent years, there have been two radical alternative proposals advanced which would deny any direct connection whatsoever between the book of the law and the Pentateuch. First of all, Rendtorff has tried to argue that there is a great difference between the law with which Ezra was sent to Jerusalem in Ezra 7.12ff. and the law which he is said in Ezra 7.10 to have studied and in Neh. 8 to have read to the people. In the Aramaic of Artaxerxes' edict, the word used is *dāt*. Rendtorff maintains that elsewhere this word is always used of the civil law of the king, and that it has no religious overtones. It is only in the later editorial stages of the books' composition that this was (mistakenly) identified with the *tôrāh*, the Jewish religious law embodied in the Pentateuch.

Two points may be made in response to this suggestion. First, the word *dāt* seems to have explicit religious overtones when it occurs as a loan-word in Hebrew at Esth. 3.8 and more especially in the Aramaic text of Dan. 6.5, where Daniel's enemies seek to trap him in a charge of disloyalty to the king on the basis of 'the law of his God'. In both these verses, it is most probable that the writers had the Mosaic law in mind. Second, Rendtorff does not suggest what alternative Aramaic word might have been used by Artaxerxes had he wished to refer more explicitly to the Jewish law. *dāt* is an Iranian loan-word, and as such it may well have developed wider meanings in its new languages of Aramaic and Hebrew than it originally had. The context must determine its significance. In this connection, Ezra 7.25, with its talk of 'the law of your God and the law of the king', seems most likely to imply the two separate but (in Artaxerxes' view) complementary spheres of religious and civil law.

The second new proposal which deserves mention is that of Houtman. His concern is not just with Ezra's law book but with that referred to in the books of Ezra and Nehemiah as a whole. After surveying the various laws which are said to derive from it, he finds that a number have no counterpart in the Pentateuch. He therefore concludes that this law book must be some quite separate work. As an analogy for the kind of work which he has in mind, Houtman cites the recently published Temple Scroll from Qumran. Though having some relationship with the Pentateuch, this scroll also 'makes clear that it was evidently customary up to late times to compile new collections of laws with the help of laws of Moses already known' (p. 110). The law book of Ezra and Nehemiah thus has 'a character of its own which is not transmitted to us' (p. 109).

Naturally, the nature of Houtman's theory is such that it cannot be disproved beyond all doubt. Nevertheless it seems improbable, and it is not necessary, in my view, as an explanation for the observations which he has made. First, the analogy with the Temple Scroll is not exact, because the Scroll purports to be a first-person address by God himself. It cannot, therefore, be used as evidence for the opinion that 'there were circles of men who held themselves entitled to promulgate existing laws anew in the name of Moses . . . and to add new laws . . . and to establish new rules' (p. 110). Second, it seems most unlikely that 'the book of the Law of Moses which the Lord had commanded for Israel' (Neh. 8.1) should have been quite separate from the Pentateuch in view of the latter's significance in the formation of Judaism. The post-exilic community was not a break-away sect like the people of Qumran. That the law on which the restoration was based should have been lost without trace while the Pentateuch, unmentioned here on this view, should have silently risen to its place of supreme authority, seems an extraordinary hypothesis.

How, then, are we to explain the apparent discrepancies between the text of the Pentateuch and the citations in Ezra and Nehemiah? It may be suggested that an explanation lies in the methods which Ezra and others applied in the interpretation of the older law and its application to the new circumstances of their own day. And to this important area we must therefore now turn.

2. The Interpretation of the Law

If the law book which the post-exilic community accepted as authoritative was the Pentateuch, two major problems confronted them as they sought to regulate their lives by it. First, several law-codes are embedded in the Pentateuch, and on some matters it is not immediately clear how their various demands are to be related to each other. Second, the circumstances of the later community differed in a number of significant ways from the earlier nation for which the laws were originally drafted. The laws could not, therefore, always be applied in a literal or direct manner.

In a brief but extremely helpful article, Clines has made a particular study of Neh. 10 in order to determine the methods which were used to overcome these difficulties. There is no need to repeat here all of Clines's observations, but a few examples may be given to illustrate the thrust of his analysis.

Sometimes, in order to ensure that an existing law was properly kept, it was necessary to create or to update a 'facilitating law'. For instance, Lev. 6.8-13 prescribes that the fire on the altar of sacrifice should be kept continually burning. (In the wording of Neh. 10.34, it is clearly to this that the phrase 'as it is written in the law' refers.) In order to facilitate obedience to this demand, the community established a 'wood offering', to ensure that sufficient fuel was always available (Neh. 10.34; cf. 13.31). (Previously, this had been the responsibility of the Gibeonites, according to Josh. 9.27, but that no longer obtained after the exile.) It follows that there is no need to look for a specific Pentateuchal reference to a 'wood offering', as Houtman implies. In cases where different laws in the Pentateuch appear to compete with one another, they tended to be harmonized by a process of integration and accumulation. For example, the various laws about taxes were all to be observed: one did not replace another. Hence Neh. 10.35-39 compounds first fruits, prime produce and tithes, the community accepting the obligation to pay them all.

As a final example, we may take the development of the laws about debt-release and the seven-year cycle of a 'Sabbath' for the land to illustrate how one requirement came to be interpreted in the light of another. On the one hand we have the law which required that all land should lie fallow for one year in seven, and that the poor should be allowed to enjoy the benefit of any produce which grew upon it (Exod. 23.10-11). There is no evidence that this was to be observed simultaneously throughout the country: most likely it was practised originally in rotation. Later, however, the view developed that one year in seven should be observed simultaneously throughout the land (Lev. 25.1-7; 2 Chron. 36.21). On the other hand, there was a separate law which was also tied to a seven-year cycle, namely the release of Israelites who had become slaves, probably because of debt (Exod. 21.2-6). Originally, this presumably meant that an Israelite slave was to be set free after he had served for six years, but the later Deut. 15.1-18 shows that in time a universal seven-year cycle developed so that any who were enslaved part way through the cycle would in fact get away with a shorter period of service.

With a comparable development thus affecting both sets of laws, it was not surprising that the question of their mutual relationship came to be raised. Neh. 10.31b shows clearly that the post-exilic community understood that they were to be taken together, the legislation being again regarded as cumulative rather than alternative.

This type of reflection on the mass of Pentateuchal legislation in the light of developing circumstances was to continue and grow for many centuries, and the much later Mishnah and Talmud are impressive testimonies to the fertile exegetical labour which it entailed. But how did this process begin? Where does the development of new law codes cease and the task of reinterpretation and application of existing authoritative law begin? We may suggest that this was one of the great legacies of Ezra himself, as two examples, not treated in Clines's more restricted investigation, suggest.

In Ezra 9.1-2 the legal basis for the dissolution of mixed marriages is set out. Though not attributed directly to Ezra himself, it is almost certain that it reflects the impact of his teaching.

Marriage with foreigners in itself is not forbidden in the Pentateuch, and indeed it includes a number of examples of such marriages (e.g. Gen. 16.3; 41.45; Exod. 2.21; Num. 12.1). The particular danger was, however, recognized that marriage with the indigenous population of Canaan would almost certainly lead to religious apostasy (Exod. 34.11-16; Deut. 7.1-4; 20.10-18), and so these were expressly forbidden.

In Ezra 9.1 we can see how, once conditions had changed beyond the point where the law could be applied literally, its principle was nevertheless upheld. Three points should be noted:

(i) First, laws dealing with the indigenous population of Canaan are now interpreted to refer to the contemporary 'peoples of the lands'. Ethnically there was no exact equation, but the intention of the law that the chief religious danger comes from those closest at hand is accurately represented. We may note, however, that the text does not identify 'the peoples of the lands' as Canaanites etc. The list of peoples (several long since extinct) at the end of the verse qualifies the word 'abominations', and is thus being used as a stereotyped legal formula. We are thus justified in speaking here of an interpretation of the earlier text.

(ii) At this point, the interpretation keeps in step with the law in regarding the evil of a mixed marriage as being religious, not racial. The Israelite partner is led astray 'according to the abominations of the Canaanites'.

(iii) The list of peoples at the end of Ezra 9.1 has no exact parallel in the Pentateuch. It is apparently an accumulation from two separate passages—Deut. 7.1 and 23.3. We thus have an example of the drawing together of comparable scriptures and of the one reflecting on the other, for in fact, unlike Deut. 7, Deut. 23 actually says nothing about inter-marriage. This process is further extended by the addition of Egyptians to the list. In all probability this testifies to the drawing in of yet a further passage in the law, Lev. 18. This chapter, which deals with all manner of forbidden marriages, is introduced in v. 3 by the words, 'After the doings of the land of Egypt in which you dwelt you shall not do; and after the doings of the land of Canaan, whither I am bringing you, you shall not do'.

If we feel reasonably comfortable with this interpretation of the law so far, Ezra 9.2 takes things a step further in a manner which we may regard as unjustified. After a citation of Deut. 7.3 there follows what appears to be an appeal to the laws of holiness which forbade the 'mixing' of unlike crops, animals or material (Lev. 19.19). This makes it look as though the community is now regarding itself as racially distinct from its neighbours, an impression reinforced by the phrase 'holy seed'. This is an unprecedented combination of the Deuteronomic concept of a 'holy nation' with the frequent use of the phrase 'seed of Abraham', influenced, no doubt, by the related verb 'to sow seed' in Lev. 19.19.

If all this seems more than usually confusing, the reason is that it is! What matters to us for the moment is to appreciate how several originally quite separate laws are being brought into combination with each other in order to establish new guidelines for the life of the people.

Our second example is more straightforward. In Neh. 8.13-18 we have the description of a celebration of the Feast of Tabernacles following on from a careful study of the law (v. 13). Amongst other things, we are told that 'they found written in the law which the Lord had commanded through Moses, that the Israelites should live in booths during the feast of the seventh month, and that they should proclaim the following words and spread them throughout their cities and Jerusalem: "Go out into the hill country and bring branches of olive and oleaster, of myrtle, palm and leafy trees in order to make booths, as prescribed"' (vv. 14-15). The problem here is that this is not an exact citation from the Pentateuch. Once again, two points need to be taken together in order to arrive at a solution.

First, the passage in general must be referring to Lev. 23, since that is the only place where the erection of booths is explicitly mentioned (cf. Lev. 23.42). The introduction to this chapter, however, states twice that 'these are the set feasts . . . which you shall proclaim in their appointed season' (vv. 2 and 4). Not unnaturally, it will have been asked what exactly they were supposed to proclaim, and Neh. 8.15 supplies the answer. It is a further case of Ezra making the law relevant for the people of his own day.

Second, there is a clear implication that the proclamation summoned the people to Jerusalem. While there is no mention of this in Lev. 23, it will have been a natural deduction from Deut. 16.15, where the feast was to be celebrated 'in the place which the Lord shall choose'. Here, then, is another case of one passage being brought to bear on the interpretation of another, of 'scripture interpreting scripture'.

These two examples will suffice to illustrate how Ezra succeeded in breathing new life into ancient laws that were in danger of becoming a dead letter. Against all the odds, he paved the way for the people to find their identity in, and to regulate their continuing life by, a book which from now on was ever contemporary.

Finally, it may be noted that he was especially concerned to ensure that it should be available to all the people and not just be the preserve of the experts. It is surely significant that his presentation took place not in the temple, but in an open space in front of the Water Gate (Neh. 8.1 and 3). To this public place could come the whole 'congregation, both men and women, and all that could hear with understanding' (probably children). Moreover, his aim as he

read is explicitly stated to have been that they should all understand
(vv. 8 and 12). The law was here being presented as something which
could indeed serve as a foundation for the life of the community. And
lest we are tempted to suppose that this was purely a concern of the
historical Ezra, let it be remembered that the editor used Neh. 8 to
introduce his major climax to the whole process of restoration and
reformation, and that he closed this major section with the account
in Neh. 10 of how the whole community (10.28 echoes 8.2!) willingly
bound themselves to observe this law in general (v. 29) and to keep in
particular a number of specific stipulations which show how they
had taken to heart the principles of exegesis which Ezra had first
introduced.

Further Reading

The articles of Houtman and Kellermann in particular include extensive
summaries of earlier research on the question of the identification of Ezra's
law book.

D.J.A. Clines, 'Nehemiah 10 as an Example of Early Jewish
    Biblical Exegesis', *JSOT* 21 (1981), 111-17

M. Fishbane, *Biblical Interpretation in Ancient Israel*, Oxford:
    Clarendon, 1985

C. Houtman, 'Ezra and the Law', *OTS* 21 (1981), 91-115

In der Smitten, *Esra*, 124-30.

U. Kellermann, 'Erwägungen zum Esragesetz', *ZAW* 80 (1968),
    373-85

Mowinckel, *Studien III*, 124-41 (Amongst other things, Mowinckel
    makes the important point that there is no reason to
    suppose that Ezra's law was previously unknown to the
    Judaean community)

Von Rad, *Das Geschichtsbild des Chronistischen Werkes*, 38-63

R. Rendtorff, 'Esra und das "Gesetz"', *ZAW* 96 (1984), 165-84

J.G. Vink, 'The Date and Origin of the Priestly Code in the Old
    Testament', *OTS* 15 (1969), 1-144

Widengren, 'The Persian Period', 514-15

INDEXES

INDEX OF PRINCIPAL PASSAGES DISCUSSED

INDEX OF SUBJECTS

INDEX OF AUTHORS

DATE DUE